"*Love*—he has to be kidding—<del>b</del>⁣⁣⁣⁣⁣⁣⁣⁣⁣⁣⁣⁣ s written an extraordinary acco⁣⁣⁣⁣⁣ r what we are doing when we say we believe in God. In doing so he has avoided the great enemies of any attempt to write about love—that is, sentimentality and rationalism. His chapter on friendship alone is worth the price of the book. I cannot help but believe that this book is destined to become a classic."

— *Stanley Hauerwas*
Duke Divinity School

"I make it a point to read at least one 'introduction to Christianity' book each year, to remind myself of what it is I believe (or want to believe). This one is as beautiful and beguiling an example of the genre as I have seen. It is humble, not assuming it has a right to your attention but seeking instead to invite your curiosity. It is generous and ecumenical, yielding space to voices like those of St. Catherine of Siena, Dorothy Day, and Dr. King. In our day of shrill and overheated religious grandstanding, its quiet witness to the God of cruciform love made me want to become a Christian all over again."

—*Wesley Hill*
Trinity School for Ministry

"In his compelling and well-written book, Bauerschmidt seeks to revitalize the affirmation that 'God is love itself.' His argument will resonate especially with those who struggle to see how Christianity matters in this postmodern world. He shows how this love is actualized in the death and resurrection of Jesus, a love shared by the friends of Jesus who gather in Spirit-created communities of care and service. Bauerschmidt's is a persuasive apologetic for the power and practicality of the core Christian message."

— *Richard Peace*
Fuller Theological Seminary

"Edifying, uplifting, instructive—these are the words that came to mind reading *The Love That Is God*. Frederick Bauerschmidt's book is a spiritual and theological meditation on the radical claim that God is love—

presented through the stories and images of the Scriptures and the wisdom of the church's beloved teachers: Augustine, Catherine of Siena, Julian of Norwich, John Chrysostom, Richard of St. Victor, Thomas Aquinas, Thérèse of Lisieux, Dorothy Day."

— Robert Louis Wilken
University of Virginia

"Drawing upon a rich variety of sources from Scripture and tradition, Bauerschmidt has written an exquisite meditation on five essential elements of the Christian faith. It combines erudition with a beautiful simplicity of expression, which will make its insights accessible and illuminating in many educational contexts: college, university, and seminary instruction, pastoral ministry, and catechetics. This little book would also make a lovely gift of inspired spiritual reading for any Christian to savor again and again."

— Kelley Spoerl
Saint Anselm College

"What is love, and how does it work? The opening words of this relevant book's introduction provide a key to how to be a Christian in our times: 'Being a Christian is difficult . . . difficult because love that goes all the way to the cross is difficult.' Bauerschmidt describes obstacles to loving and to being a Christian in our current culture and churches. Read slowly and seriously, this book can change our personal lives, renew our churches, and hopefully have a profound effect on our digital and oppressive culture. This book could help heal our painful polarizations. Heartfelt love (from and for God, ourselves, and others) is what we can believe, and how we are to live. Bauerschmidt makes this exceptionally clear and comprehensible for all."

— Dean Borgman
Gordon-Conwell Theological Seminary

The Love That Is God

An Invitation to Christian Faith

Frederick Christian Bauerschmidt

WILLIAM B. EERDMANS PUBLISHING COMPANY
GRAND RAPIDS, MICHIGAN

Wm. B. Eerdmans Publishing Co.
4035 Park East Court SE, Grand Rapids, Michigan 49546
www.eerdmans.com

27 26 25 24   7 8 9 10

ISBN 978-0-8028-7795-6

Library of Congress Cataloging-in-Publication Data

Names: Bauerschmidt, Frederick Christian, author.
Title: The love that is God : an invitation to Christian faith / Frederick
    Christian Bauerschmidt.
Description: Grand Rapids, Michigan : William B. Eerdmans Pub-
    lishing Company, 2020. | Includes bibliographical references. |
    Summary: "A brief introduction to Christianity in five statements
    of belief"—Provided by publisher.
Identifiers: LCCN 2020003719 | ISBN 9780802877956 (paperback)
Subjects: LCSH: God (Christianity)—Love. | Love—Religious aspects—
    Christianity. | Christian life.
Classification: LCC BT140 .B385 2020 | DDC 231/.6—dc23
LC record available at https://lccn.loc.gov/2020003719

For Thomas, Sophie, and Denis

God on the Cross—is the fearful hidden meaning behind this symbol still understood?

—Friedrich Nietzsche,
The Anti-Christ, 51

Contents

Foreword

This is a book that you should read, regardless of whether you are a professed Christian, a "seeker," or a skeptic. Let me explain why.

There was a time at the turn of the twentieth century when European theologians were particularly concerned about what constituted the "essence of Christianity." In part, this urgency was spurred by the increasingly felt pressure on the Christian churches at that time of the truth claims of the so-called other world religions, now increasingly seen as rivals to Christianity's "absoluteness"; and it was doubtless not a coincidence that this moment also signaled (as we can see in retrospect) the beginning of a loss of colonial confidence about the missionizing of all political subjects to the Christian faith. Yet in 1900 the great liberal German historical theologian Adolf von Harnack gave his famous lectures entitled *Das Wesen des Christentums (What Is Christianity?)*,[1] delivered extempore to a huge audience in Berlin; and when translated into myriad languages, copies of the text were said—by Paul Tillich in lectures to a later generation of students—to have blocked up the shunting yards of German railways, so busy were they transporting them all over the world.

1. Adolf von Harnack, *What Is Christianity?*, trans. Thomas Bailey Saunders (German orig. 1900; London: Williams & Norgate, 1901).

But perhaps this was the last moment in modern Western theology when it was thought possible to encapsulate the Christian theological heritage in such a succinct historical manner which claimed to probe to its unique biblical "kernel" (the teaching of Jesus on the "Fatherhood of God and the brotherhood of Man," according to Harnack). An immediate Catholic rejoinder, from the modernist Alfred Loisy,[2] understandably insisted on the need to give a much more organic and evolutionary account of the Christian faith, and indeed of the developing and branching institutional life of the church; a critical German Protestant riposte, from Harnack's rival (and later Berlin colleague) Ernst Troeltsch,[3] questioned more probingly whether the very idea of the "essence of Christianity" was covertly a *relativistic* notion: "To define the essence is to shape it afresh," he averred. Troeltsch's views were prescient of developments in Western philosophy which were to follow not much later in the twentieth century: thus, Ludwig Wittgenstein was soon to question whether the busy search for metaphysical "essences" might not be a mistaken quest, when a more fluid account of "family resemblances" between different manifestations of a complex phenomenon could do better philosophical work.[4]

2. Alfred Loisy, *The Gospel and the Church*, trans. Christopher Home (French orig. 1902; New York: Scribner, 1912).

3. Ernst Troeltsch, "What Is the Meaning of 'The Essence of Christianity'?" (German orig., 1902, rev. 1913), in *Ernst Troeltsch: Essays on Theology and Religion*, ed. and trans. Robert Morgan and Michael Pye (London: Duckworth, 1977).

4. Ludwig Wittgenstein, *Philosophical Investigations*, trans. G. E. M.

This was not to say, of course, that Catholic and Protestant churches did not continue to purvey their classical catechisms, and indeed, in due course to rewrite them for a new genera-tion in hopes of regaining some fresh dogmatic certainty to purvey to an increasingly "secularized" public. Others occa-sionally wrote succinct commentaries on the creeds or made the attempt to résumé core New Testament teaching.[5] But if "essentializing" the faith had inevitably begun to be seen as a rearguard action in the face of postmodernity's erosions of sta-bility, it did not mean that the task of giving a limpid, alluring personal account of "the hope that is in one" (1 Pet. 3:15) had any less spiritual importance.

So when we are drawn into a little book as elegant and powerful as Bauerschmidt's *The Love That Is God*, we see that he has revivified, and indeed transformed, a genre of writ-ing of which many have despaired. And even then, Bauer-schmidt's achievement and style are entirely his own. Re-sisting (but never mentioning) the tired disjunction between "liberal" and "conservative" Christianity, Bauerschmidt sets out to give his own fresh account of what *really matters* in the

---

Anscombe (German orig. 1953; London: Blackwell, 1958), see paras. 65ff. (but cp. also paras. 371, 373) on "family resemblances" and "essences."

5. There have of course nonetheless been a number of memora-ble—but extraordinarily divergent—attempts in the second part of the twentieth century to give an account of the core faith of Christianity in short compass: C. S. Lewis, Austin Farrer, John Stott, and Hans Küng immediately come to mind, and (more recently) N. T. Wright and Rowan Williams. It is interesting that so many of these are Anglican thinkers, Anglicanism being a tradition that has often smarted under the critique that it lacked a clear doctrinal core.

Bible and Christian tradition, and how it changes everything for those willing to respond to the call and demand of "the love that is God."

Why is Bauerschmidt's achievement so striking? A number of distinctive features should be mentioned.

First, it is important to read this book backwards (so to speak), because the remarkable sermon that originally inspired its fuller exposition is found at the end of the book, in lilting, indeed haunting, *poetic* form. One should read this sermon first, then; but then read it again as the fitting climax to the preceding five-chapter reflection, which is already encoded in the sermon but which demands more extended reflection on each major theme sketched out there. But it is not for nothing that this final exordium is what it is: a prose-poem-sermon that conveys, affectively, even more than it explicitly says. As such, it proves once more that the Word spoken and preached and prayed is always more than the sum of its parts. And Bauerschmidt is a fine preacher of the Word.

Then secondly, this is a book with a singular mode of discourse in its other chapters, although it takes a while to realize how unusual its combination of factors really is. It is thoroughgoingly and refreshingly biblical (and with that, Christocentric) in its core exposition, even while Bauerschmidt also takes as read the core conciliar doctrines of the faith as expounded by some of the greatest Christian theologians both West and East, who are liberally and illuminatingly cited. Yet each chapter is also woven around a set of skeptical or questioning interlocutions—the "voices off," one suspects, of Bauerschmidt's undergraduate students, young adults, and sometimes disillusioned friends. One of the reasons the text is so fresh and attractive, then, is that doubts and disturbances about the faith and its institutions are so seriously and charitably addressed—indeed, treated as issues that no responsible believer would want to sweep aside. At the same time, the reader is invited into a deeper place of reflection than mere ratiocination about doctrinal difficulties: prayer and practice are at the heart of the exposition, and each chapter turns to the mystics and social reformers who have embodied such an integration. Indeed, a remarkable Christian woman is chosen in the case of each major point of discussion to exemplify this challenge and possibility.

This is a book that you will find hard to put down, then, even if you disagree with it. That is why you should read and ponder it yourself, and give it to your children and your godchildren, and recommend it to your friends who have tired of institutional Christianity, and your atheist acquaintances who like to fulminate against the very idea of God, and especially a God who was crucified. If Bauerschmidt has "defined the essence" by "shaping it afresh" (in Troeltsch's terms), then the new freshness of his "shaping" has produced its own reward. But more important still is the clear challenge to *live* what is here propounded. As the book ends:

> "That is it.
> That is what Christianity is all about.
> Now believe it and live it
> as if your life depended on it,
> because it does."

Introduction

Being a Christian is difficult. It is difficult because love that goes all the way to the cross is difficult, both to receive and to give. It has always been difficult, though at different times and places that difficulty has been felt in different ways. In our own time and place, the postindustrial West, difficulties include those arising from the nature of the modern world that make Christian claims seem in-credible: a narrowed understanding of truth, suspicion of traditions, ever-increasing individualism. Difficulties also arise from the failures of Christians: scandals, bigotries, the banal reduction of mystery to moralism and of morality to modes of social conformity. This book attempts to make the case that the difficulties are worth it. It is worth the difficult labor of piercing through the barriers of our own assumptions and looking beyond the unlovely face that Christians often show to the world, because the fundamental affirmations of Christianity can be a source of love and joy and meaning, even amid the difficulty.

There are, of course, many different ways in which one might articulate the fundamental affirmations of Christianity. That is more or less what various different creeds try to do, and I don't have any aspiration to replace the traditional creeds of Christianity, which remain an indispensable communal grammar of belief. What I offer here is simply one attempt to speak of Christian faith to people of my time and place in a way that might convey some of the attractive force of things that lie at the heart of the life and teachings of Jesus. In particular, I wish to show how the claim that the love that is God is crucified love offers us a way to understand how the joys and sorrows of our existence can be enfolded within the eternal love that is our source.

The idea for this book arose after I preached a sermon that I have included as the epilogue of this book, where I tried to sketch in five points what I took to be the heart of the Christianity: God is love; the love that is God is crucified love; we are called to friendship with the risen Jesus; we cannot love God if we do not love each other; and we live out our love from the community created by the Spirit. At the end of church, a friend said that she liked the sermon and wished her daughter, who had little time for the church, could have been there to hear it. I began thinking that I wished my own children, members of that same generation of young people who are highly suspicious of Christianity, could have been there to hear it as well (not that they haven't heard plenty from me over the years). I began to think about how to convey the truth and power that the Christian faith contains to people, whether young or old, who desire a more just and equitable world, who seek to live lives of kindness and compassion, who want more from life than simply employment punctuated by entertainment, but who are pretty sure that Christianity has nothing to say to any of those desires. I also wanted to speak a word of encouragement to those who do feel that Christianity has something to say to our deepest desires, but wonder how to articulate what that thing is.

Communication is irreducibly mysterious, and its success is often beyond our control. I generally feel that the most important things ever said to me were inadvertent or offhand remarks from the perspective of those who said them. Who can possibly know what the right thing is to say, particularly when one speaks of God? Near the end of his life, following a profound religious experience while celebrating Mass, Thomas Aquinas ceased writing. He is reported to have said, when asked why he had ceased his theological labors, "All that I have written seems like straw to me compared with what I have seen." As Thomas himself had often said, the inadequacy of human language plagues all attempts to talk about God. But sometimes even our straw can be used by God as tinder upon which the spark of the Spirit can fall. If I can convey some small measure of the joy and truth that lie at the heart of faith, this will not be due to any skill or eloquence on my part, but to the compelling beauty of crucified love.

God is love.

A witty and pugnacious atheist, the late English writer Christopher Hitchens once described the statement "God is love" as "white noise": a sentimental bit of propaganda designed to trick the simpleminded into thinking that religion is a benign force. This phrase, found in the New Testament's first letter of John (4:8), certainly has been trivialized, ensconced in bubble letters on posters with puppies to induce warm fuzzies. It is also abused by Christians who use it to distract onlookers from the fact that they have their foot planted firmly on someone else's neck or to manipulate people into thinking that some violation of human dignity is being done out of love of God.

Trivialization and abuse can lead us to forget that the claim that God is love is *the* radical claim of Christianity. It is radical not simply in the sense of being a shocking or explosive claim, but in the sense of lying at the root (Latin *radix*) of the Christian faith. In some sense, the entirety of things that Christians believe flows from this claim. It is a belief that distinguished Christianity from much ancient imagining of the divine, whether in the mythological form of tales of the gods or the philosophical form of reflection on the source of universal order. It is anticipated by the ancient Israelite understanding of a God who enters into a covenant with Abraham and his descendants, a covenant grounded in God's steadfast love, but even there, where loving-kindness for creation characterizes God, we find nothing quite as audacious as the claim that God *is* love.

*   *   *

But is this claim credible? The notion that God is love suggests that something of what it means to believe in God can be gleaned from what it means to believe oneself to be loved. In discussing what faith is and is not, I often ask the students I teach whether they believe that their parents love them. This is, of course, a risky strategy since there is a not-insignificant number of people who are unsure whether they are loved by their parents (or by anyone, for that matter). But at least a few of them will admit that they believe that their parents love them. I then press the case: would they say that they *believe* this, or would they say that they *know* this? Do they believe it in the sense that they believe that LeBron James is the greatest basketball player of all time or that housing prices will go down, or do they believe it perhaps in the sense that they believe that George Washington was the first president of the United States or that energy equals mass times the speed of light squared? We use the word *believe* in a variety of ways: sometimes to state a preference or to make a guess about something unknowable (both of which we describe as "having an opinion") and at other times to say that we hold fast to what we have learned from someone we judge to be in a position to know or that we grasp a truth with certainty for ourselves (both of which we typically describe as "knowing"). Which of these sorts of things is the statement "I believe my parents love me" more like?

It doesn't seem like a mere opinion. To say that I believe my parents love me is not like saying, "I like the idea of my parents loving me" or "I think my parents love me, but I very well might be wrong; who can possibly know?" But it also doesn't seem exactly like knowledge. I am not simply accepting someone's authoritative statement, as if I were to say, "I accept that my parents love me because nine out of ten scientists agree that they do"; nor am I claiming to apprehend something that could not possibly be otherwise, like a mathematical truth. And yet to believe that one is loved by one's parents is at least as fundamental to one's actual being-in-the-world as any number of facts that we would ordinarily claim to know. It's a truth that in a very real sense we stake our lives on.

I suggest to my students that believing they are loved by their parents is unlike an opinion in that it presumes some evidence, but it is also unlike knowledge in that it is not something we accept because we possess unshakable proof. In other words, this belief falls somewhere between opinion and knowledge. When I ask what sorts of evidence they can present for this belief, my students mention things like the financial sacrifices their parents have made for their education, the clear happiness with which they are greeted when they return home, or the care packages they receive during the exam period. Couldn't these things, I ask in reply, all be part of an elaborate ruse, perhaps a plot to lull them into a sense of false security so their parents can murder them in their sleep and collect insurance money on them? But, they object, they have been doing these things for a long time with no sign of malicious intent. Perhaps, I suggest, they are patiently working the long con, stringing them along and gaining their trust so that they will let their guard down.

At this point, the students begin to scoff, and rightly so, because the alternative that I must construct to account for their sense of their parents' love is so absurdly elaborate that it becomes incredible—not worthy of belief. They cannot absolutely demonstrate that my incredible alternative is false, but it is not capable of shaking the conviction born of a lifetime of converging probabilities. Though something like parental love is not subject to empirical verification, they are still willing to affirm its reality. Indeed, until I ruthlessly badger them in the classroom, it has never occurred to most of them that they might need reasons for that affirmation. It is so basic that, though they can come up with reasons on the fly when pressed, they ordinarily would feel no need to make an argument for it. And it is in this sense that we might call it a "bedrock" affirmation. It is a presumption that we use to make sense of the world. Such a bedrock affirmation is what the nineteenth-century theologian John Henry Newman called "certitude" (as opposed to certainty), which is "the result of an *assemblage* of concurring and converging probabilities" (*Apologia pro Vita Sua*, chap. 1).

Philosophy may or may not be able to prove or disprove God's existence—philosophers differ among themselves on this—but for the vast majority of believers the existence of God is not a result of philosophical proof. Some people are inclined or impelled by their own particular intellectual makeup to seek a clearly demonstrative argument for God's existence, perhaps based on the contingency of existence or the need for a ground for our moral claims or something else. Many, however, do not seek such a demonstration, simply intuiting that there must be a reason why there is something rather than nothing or that moral principles are rooted in some sort of transcendent values. But even people who do not seek demonstrations for God's existence still have reasons or motives for their belief in God, though these reasons may be less like premises in a logical argument and more like a pattern of probabilities that we take in at a glance, sometimes without even knowing that we are doing it. In either case, the important thing to note is that faith in God is not the affirmation of a neutral fact about the world, like asserting that there is an as-yet-undiscovered planet orbiting beyond Pluto. Rather, our faith in God is, like our belief that we are loved by our parents, something upon which we stake our lives.

*   *   *

If belief in God is something upon which we stake our lives, then it matters what god we believe in. It is not enough to argue that it is reasonable to affirm God's existence in the same sense that we affirm our parents' love. For Christians, it is not simply that we believe in God with a faith that is *like* our faith in human love. Rather, we want to claim that love is so characteristic of the divine that we are warranted in saying that the God in whom we believe *is* love. But, as I noted earlier, this claim is far from universal. How might we imagine a world in which the gods are real but are not the God of love?

"The Knight's Tale," the first of Geoffrey Chaucer's *Canterbury Tales*, is, among other things, the story of all-too-human lovers in a world of unloving gods. Written in the fourteenth century, it is an oddly anachronistic tale set in the world of pagan antiquity but reflecting many of the conventions of medieval courtly love literature. Two noble cousins from Thebes, Arcita and Palamon, fall in love with the same girl, Emily, whom they have observed only from afar. The love of each for her is so intense that it fractures their love for each other, making them bitter rivals, sacrificing the good of their friendship for an as-yet-unconsummated passion. Emily's brother-in-law Theseus, the Duke of Athens, decides to resolve the conflict by setting a contest of arms between the cousins. The night before the contest, Arcita, Palamon, and Emily each goes to a temple to pray: Arcita goes to the temple of Mars, the god of war, to pray for victory in the contest so that he might win Emily; Palamon goes to the temple of Venus, goddess of love, to pray that he might have Emily; Emily goes to the temple of Diana, virgin goddess of the hunt, to pray that she might remain unmarried, but she also prays that, should that prove impossible, she should be married to the one who desires her more.

These prayers occasion a great conflict among the gods since each wants to be the one who shows that he or she can deliver the goods for their petitioner. Saturn, an ancient and somewhat terrifying deity, intervenes in the squabble and shows how each god can grant what has been asked. Arcita wins the contest, just as he asked, but Saturn startles his horse, which throws him to the ground so that he dies before he can marry Emily. Palamon eventually gets to marry Emily, as he asked, as part of a deal intended to improve relations between Thebes and Athens, though his heart is permanently wounded by the loss of his cousin Arcita. Emily does not get to remain a virgin—her plan A—but she (presumably) gets her plan B: the one who loved her more (though it is not really clear how much either actually loves her as opposed to being obsessed with the idea of her). So the gods get to show their capacity to grant what is requested of them, to fulfill their roles in the transaction between humans and the divine, though at the end of the day none of the human characters seems particularly happy. The final moral of the story, delivered by Duke Theseus, seems to be that while there might be an overarching providence guiding the universe, the gods, for the most part, do not care about human happiness, and so the best we can do is "to make a virtue of necessity" ("Knight's Tale," line 3042), to accept what fate sends us and make the best of things.

Though Chaucer was a Christian, in the tale told by his knight he attempts to inhabit a pre-Christian worldview, in which the world is ruled by gods who see each other as rivals and who don't have much interest in human affairs except to the degree that they might be used to gain advantage over the other gods. The gods determine the fates of Arcita, Palamon, and Emily, but they do so in such a way that only the gods are winners. By sticking strictly to the specific way in which each of the petitioners phrases his or her prayer, the gods are able to fulfill the letter of those petitions without granting any of them what they most desire. Chaucer's description of their temples, which are filled with images of violence and misery, shows the true nature of the gods. Mars's temple, perhaps predictably, is filled with depictions of treachery and anger and fear:

> Stark War, with open wounds, all bebloodied;
> Discord, with dripping knife and direful face.
> And full of screeching was that gruesome place.
> (lines 2002-4)

But even the temple of Venus, goddess of love, depicts

> The broken sleeps and the cold sighs
> The sacred tears and the lamenting
> The fiery strokes of the desirings
> That Love's servants in this life endure.
> (lines 1920-23)

And the overarching providence that Theseus invokes at the end of the tale seems fairly indifferent to the fate of individuals as long as things as a whole turn out okay.

The depiction of human love in the tale is not much happier. The passion that Arcita and Palamon feel for Emily not only turns them against each other but has a narcissistic quality that seems totally unrelated to Emily as a flesh-and-blood reality. (Chaucer's metaphors for her are all drawn from flowers; she doesn't even get to be a warm-blooded animal.) Their love at first sight is an emotion that, for all its obsessive fervor, is free from any concern for the actual flourishing of the beloved; neither of them seems at all concerned that Emily would prefer to remain unmarried, if they even know this, since they have never bothered to have a conversation with her. And when love is finally victorious in the end, it takes the form of a marriage that is bought at the cost of Arcita's life and is engineered in order to advance political aims. The gods may be supremely loveless, but the human characters give them a run for their money.

Perhaps in writing "The Knight's Tale" Chaucer just wanted to tell a good story with action, romance, tragedy, and maybe a dash of philosophical reflection. But beneath the surface of this romance there lurks, as so often with Chaucer, a serious critique. His target is not really the religions of antiquity, which had complexities and nuances beyond the loveless gods depicted in the story told by the knight. Rather, his tale shows what the world looks like in any time and place, even—perhaps especially—among Christians, if one is unconvinced that God is love.

If God is not love, then the divine forces at work in the world are simply out for themselves, unconcerned with our well-being or only concerned with it to the degree that it advances their own self-aggrandizing agenda.

If God is not love, then whatever providential impulse there is that might be leading the universe as a whole to a favorable outcome does not particularly care about this or that individual; rather history appears to be, as Hegel put it, "the slaughter-bench at which the happiness of peoples, the wisdom of States, and the virtue of individuals have been victimized" (*Philosophy of History*, 21).

If God is not love, then the best we human beings can manage is love as a passion at war with goodness, at war with friendship and with seeking the good of the beloved, so that all our loves are marked by a rivalry that gives birth to a violence that will be contained only by concerns for political expediency.

*   *   *

Even if we believe that God *is* love, we still must ask, "What then is love?" Is it the passion felt by Arcita and Palamon for Emily? Is it the care of parents shown to children of which my students are so certain? We use the word *love* like we use the word *believe*, in a number of different ways. Pope Benedict XVI, in his 2005 encyclical letter *Deus caritas est* (God Is Love), notes "the vast semantic range of the word 'love': we speak of love of country, love of one's profession, love between friends, love of work, love between parents and children, love between family members, love of neighbor and love of God" (1.2). We clearly do not mean *exactly* the same thing by the word *love* in all these cases, but neither do we mean radically different things. Love of country is not exactly like love between friends, but if we have some idea of what love between friends is, this can give us some sense of what people mean when they say they love their country (it can also mislead us if we do not recognize the relevant differences). The way theologians make this point is to say that *love* is an analogical term, meaning that its sense can be extended or stretched over a disparate array of things. It is being stretched in this way by the writer of the first letter of John when he says "God is love." He is not saying that God is the feeling I have toward friends or my country or that my parents or spouse have toward me, but that these things somehow point me in the general direction of who God is.

Is it possible to be more specific? The thirteenth-century theologian Thomas Aquinas speaks of love in terms of an activity within us: "love is naturally the first act of the will and appetite." That is to say, to love is to be drawn toward something by desiring it or to delight in something by possessing it. He also speaks of love in terms of our attitude toward the object of our love: "to love a person is to wish that person good" (*Summa theologiae* 1.20.1). We might say that love is the desire for and delight in someone or something's goodness. It is a desire that delights in the sheer existence of the beloved and wants that existence to flourish. As the twentieth-century philosopher Josef Pieper put it, to love something or someone is to say "I am glad you exist" ("On Love," 164). To love my wife is to desire her and delight in the sheer fact of her existence; to love pizza is to desire and delight in pizza's existence. Of course, my desire for and delight in pizza is not exactly the same thing as my desire for and delight in my wife because what it means for my wife to flourish as a human being is something quite different from what it means for pizza to flourish as pizza. Plus, I wish for the pizza to be the best possible pizza because then it will give me the greatest pleasure; my desire for my wife's flourishing at least has the possibility of being for her own sake and not simply for my pleasure. Yet whether we are talking about a spouse or a food or a country, to love something is to, as it were, wish it well, wish that it be what it is in the fullest sense possible.

*   *   *

The fourteenth-century Englishwoman Julian of Norwich writes, "God is kind in his being: that is to say, that goodness that is kind, it is God. . . . He is the same thing that is kindness, and he is the father and mother of kinds" (*Revelations of Divine Love*, chap. 62). This Middle English word *kind* proves useful for Julian in articulating the identity of the God who is love. On the one hand, *kind* in Middle English means more or less what it means in contemporary English: an attitude of benevolence shown in our actions. On the other hand, *kind* also means a nature or species—the *kind* of thing something is, as when we might speak of humankind to denote all of those who share in human nature. To treat someone kindly it to treat them as your kinfolk, as those to whom one, in a sense, is obligated to wish well because of some common identity. Julian plays with this dual meaning of *kind* when she says that God "is the same thing that is kindness." God's kindness is shown to all the different kinds of things that exist, who are akin to God because of the existence that God generously shares with them. Julian's description of God as "the father and mother of kinds" underscores God's kinship with creatures as the source of their existence. You might say that the existence of God and the existence of creatures in all their diversity bear a family resemblance to each other, just as children bear a family resemblance to their parents, because God is the source of creaturely existence.

In other words, our first hint of the God who is love might be found in the gift of existence that we are: to know oneself to be a creature is to know that one's existence is given by God, not based on any deserving but on God's benevolence. This is precisely how God's love differs from our loves. My love, whether of my wife or of pizza, is based on some goodness that I see in the thing I love. It is my wife's intelligence and beauty and integrity that draw me to her. It is pizza's crispy and cheesy deliciousness that makes me desire it. Even things that are not obviously attractive still possess some goodness that draws us to them, if only the bare goodness of existing itself. It is perhaps the mark of the saint to be drawn in love to the unlovely simply because they are God's creatures. God's love, however, is not drawn to any goodness in us at all but rather creates the entirety of our goodness, even the goodness of bare existence itself. Julian's contemporary Catherine of Siena writes in one of her prayers, "You, eternal God, saw me and knew me in yourself. And because you saw me in your light you fell in love with your creature and drew her out of yourself and created her in your image and likeness" (Prayer 13 in O'Driscoll, *Passion for Truth*, 75). We might say that God's love is active rather than reactive, creating the creature that is the object of God's love. As Augustine wrote, addressing God, "We see these things you have made because they exist, but they exist because you see them" (*Confessions* 13.38.53).

When we realize that our very existence is the result of

God's loving us, then we are freed from the fear that God might not love us, and we begin to have some dim understanding of what it means to say that God is love itself. If God has no motive for giving us existence except love—if God gains nothing by our being, accrues no benefits—then the love that moves God to create us must simply be what God is: God is "kind." Earlier I suggested that in some sense God is not a "thing" that we investigate. To say that God is love is to say that God is not simply the kind of thing that loves but is the activity of loving itself—not our human act of love, not even the sum total of such acts, but an activity that is prior to and the source of our human being and knowing and desiring, an act of love so vast and deep that it brings forth creatures in all their diversity: ravines and rivers, sassafras and sequoias, bacteria and border collies. To say that God is love is to say that God is a benevolence, a well-wishing, a kindness of such infinite scope that it draws beloved creatures out of nothingness into being. The God who is love, as St. Paul says, "gives life to the dead and calls into existence the things that do not exist" (Rom. 4:17). If, as Josef Pieper put it, what it means for us to love someone or something is to say "I am glad you exist," then what it means for God to love us is for God to say, "Because I am glad, you exist."

*   *   *

But the belief that God is love, benevolence, or kindness should not be confused with the belief that God is "nice." As the Rev. Martin Luther King Jr. put it, "The greatness of our God lies in the fact that he is both tough minded and tenderhearted"

(*Strength to Love*, 8). The Bible gives ample evidence of a God who makes demands on people and holds them accountable, letting them suffer the consequences of their desire to live as if their existence were not God's gift. One way to interpret the story of Adam and Eve in the garden (Gen. 3) is that in tempting Adam and Eve to eat from the tree of the knowledge of good and evil, so as to "be like God," the serpent is tempting them to seek to be the source of their own existence. But, of course, we are *not* the source of our own existence, so when we declare independence from God, our existence begins to diminish, to become weak and paltry. St. Augustine writes, "To abandon God and to exist in oneself, that is to please oneself, is not immediately to lose all being; but it is to come close to nothingness" (*City of God* 14.13). God permits us to suffer this paltriness, which we experience not simply in terms of our mortality but also in our inability to align our loving with the love that is God, our inability to direct our passions and desires in ways that are life-giving. Arcita and Palamon are led to unhappy ends by their rivalrous passion for Emily, who for her part must suffer being turned from a flesh-and-blood person into a limited commodity to be fought over and, ultimately, of losing the agency of her single life for the sake of a political alliance. It is as if, bereft of belief in the God who is benevolent love, Chaucer's lovers make themselves into images of the self-seeking deities whom they worship.

Scripture attests not only to God letting us experience the consequences of our actions but also to God taking action against the wicked. The prophets of the Old Testament verbally lacerate the people of Israel in the name of God for failing to keep God's covenant of love and justice. Amos delivers the following message from the God who is love:

> I hate, I despise your festivals,
>   and I take no delight in your solemn
>   assemblies.
> Even though you offer me your burnt-offerings
>   and grain-offerings,
>   I will not accept them;
> and the offerings of well-being of your fatted
>   animals
>   I will not look upon.
> Take away from me the noise of your songs;
>   I will not listen to the melody of your harps.
> But let justice roll down like waters,
>   and righteousness like an ever-flowing
>   stream. (Amos 5:21–24)

The New Testament's book of Revelation presents a no-less-sobering vision of a divine day of reckoning:

> Then a mighty angel took up a stone like a great
>   millstone and threw it into the sea,
>   saying,
> "With such violence Babylon the great city
>   will be thrown down,
>   and will be found no more;
> and the sound of harpists and minstrels and of
>   flautists and trumpeters

> will be heard in you no more;
> and an artisan of any trade
>   will be found in you no more;
> and the sound of the millstone
>   will be heard in you no more;
> and the light of a lamp
>   will shine in you no more;
> and the voice of bridegroom and bride
>   will be heard in you no more;
> for your merchants were the magnates of the
>   earth,
>   and all nations were deceived by your
>   sorcery.
> And in you was found the blood of prophets and
>   of saints,
>   and of all who have been slaughtered on
>   earth." (Rev. 18:21–24)

To those who oppress the poor and slaughter the prophets and saints, the God of love appears as a fire consuming them like chaff.

How can we claim that God is love while at the same time saying that God allows us to suffer the consequences of our actions or, even worse, that God takes action against us because of our injustice? Can perfect love be both tough-minded and tenderhearted? Perhaps it is a matter of perspective. If we abandon the perspective of those who think they are in control and take up the perspective of those who are oppressed and defenseless, then scriptural passages like those quoted above appear a bit differently—not simply as punishment of the wicked but as divine vindication for those who have been wronged. Perhaps the full unveiling of the God of love will look and feel different to us depending on the degree to which we have aligned ourselves with that love and with those most protected, defended, and claimed by that love. The fire of love that warms and purifies also consumes and destroys; the light that illuminates can also blind. St. Catherine of Siena writes, "A healthy eye looks at the sun and sees light. But a sick eye sees nothing but darkness when it looks into such lightsomeness—and it is no fault of the light that it seems so different to the two; the fault is in the sick eye" (*Dialogue*, chap. 39). If we have narrowed our hearts, the experience of being flooded with the love that is God might painfully burst them open. But to have hope in God is to believe that no heart can be burst beyond God's power to mend.

*   *   *

The mystery of the gift of our existence, this manifestation of the God who is love in what is not God, is rooted in a still deeper mystery: the mystery of interpersonal love within God's own self, in the shared love of the Father, Son, and Holy Spirit. St. Augustine writes, "If you see love, you see the Trinity" (*De Trinitate* 8.8.12). The twelfth-century theologian Richard of St. Victor expands on this insight by reflecting on what it means to believe that God is not simply love but the greatest love. Implicitly drawing on St. Anselm's idea of God as "something than which no greater can be thought" (*Proslo-*

gion, chap. 2), Richard argues that if God is love, God must be the highest form of love that we can conceive. The greatest love, he says, is *caritas*, which is the Latin term that Western theologians used to translate the New Testament's Greek term *agapē*. This is the love that Paul writes of in his first letter to the Corinthian Christians: "Love is patient; love is kind; love is not envious or boastful or arrogant or rude. It does not insist on its own way; it is not irritable or resentful; it does not rejoice in wrongdoing, but rejoices in the truth. It bears all things, believes all things, hopes all things, endures all things" (1 Cor. 13:4–7).

Richard notes that no one is said to have this *caritas* if their love is directed solely to themselves; it must be directed to another; it must be interpersonal. Likewise, the *caritas* of God, since it is the most perfect love, must be directed toward that which is most perfect. But only God is perfect, so the love that is God cannot be directed first and foremost to created things but must be directed toward one who is God. This suggests that there must be within God a kind of "otherness," so that the love that is God might be both perfect and truly interpersonal. Richard writes, "So that the fullness of charity can occur in true divinity, it is necessary for a divine person not to lack the fellowship with a person of equal dignity and, for that reason, a divine person" (*De Trinitate* 3.2). The love that is God, if it is to be the highest sort of love, must be not just love given but also love received since "love cannot be pleasant if it is not also mutual" (3.3), as anyone who has suffered from unrequited love can attest.

Richard goes on to argue that the love that is God, as the most perfect love, must exceed even a love shared between two divine persons. Lovers can become so focused on their mutual exchange of love that they become a closed circle that excludes all others; such love can be its own kind of selfishness, an *égoïsme à deux*. So, Richard says, "the proof of perfected charity is a willing sharing of the love that has been shown you" (*De Trinitate* 3.11); the perfect love that God is must be not simply interpersonal but overflowing. As Richard puts it, "Shared love is properly said to exist when a third person is loved by two persons harmoniously and in community, and the affection of the two persons is fused into one affection by the flames of love for the third" (3.19).

Striving for deeper vision into the mystery of the God who is love, seeking the most perfect of loves, Richard draws upon the Christian understanding of God as Trinity—Father, Son, and Holy Spirit, existing eternally as one divine essence—to show how God can be the love than which no greater can be thought: an interpersonal love that comes from God and is directed toward God, fruitfully freed of all selfishness, eternally generative of still more love. The God who is love is not a "thing" but an activity. The Father is the loving of the Son, and the Son is the returning of love to the Father, and from this mutuality of love the loving that is the Holy Spirit is breathed out, the contented sigh of the eternal lovers. God is, we might say, the eternal and unconstrained play of interpersonal love, and it is from the heart of this eternal play of love that we creatures are brought forth into time and history.

In the mystery of the Trinity we glimpse the love that God is, the love that is the source of our being. Even a glimpse is enough to suggest that this love is quite different from the love—whether divine or human—that is on display in Chaucer's "Knight's Tale." There, love is either absent, as in the gods, or destructive, as it is for Arcita, Palamon, and Emily. The triune God, however, is love freed from self-seeking, from rivalry, from objectification, from the torments of passion and obsession. Unlike the trio of Mars, Venus, and Diana, the God who is Father, Son, and Spirit is interpersonal life unmarred by rivalry and self-seeking because it is grounded in the eternal act of kindness that is God's essence. This divine kindness is the endless sea of love upon which our created being floats. This is the love that can heal the failures of our human loves. Catherine of Siena concludes her work *The Dialogue* with a hymn of thanksgiving to the holy Trinity:

> You, eternal Trinity, are a deep sea: The more I enter you, the more I discover, and the more I discover, the more I seek you. You are insatiable, you in whose depth the soul is sated yet remains always hungry for you, thirsty for you, eternal Trinity, longing to see you with the light in your light. . . . With that light I sense my soul once again becoming drunk! Thanks be to God! Amen! (*Dialogue*, chap. 167)

But theological reflections on the nature of love, even those of so deep a lover of God as Richard of St. Victor, are ultimately insufficient to unveil this love for us. The true revelation of this love is found in the life, death, and resurrection of Jesus of Nazareth.

Further Reading

- The First Letter of John. The source of the statement "God is love," this New Testament letter, probably by the author of the Gospel of John and written near the end of the first century, is aimed at showing how the belief that God is love should shape the life of Christians in their interactions with each other.

- Benedict XVI, *God Is Love*. This 2005 letter from Pope Benedict XVI, addressed to the whole church, explores belief in the God who is love in a modern context, spelling out the theological, social, and political implications of this belief and addressing some modern critiques of Christian love.

2

The love that is God is crucified love.

In his encyclical letter *Deus caritas est*, Pope Benedict writes, "Being Christian is not the result of an ethical choice or a lofty idea, but the encounter with an event, a person, which gives life a new horizon and a decisive direction" (*Deus caritas est* 1). Benedict wishes to move Christian faith away from theological and moral abstractions and refocus it on a concrete person. This person—this "event"—is Jesus of Nazareth, called the Christ, the English form of the Greek translation (*Christos*) of the Hebrew word *māshîah* (Anglicized as "Messiah"), a term that means "the anointed one." In identifying Jesus as the Christ, we locate him within the context of the hope of the people Israel, the descendants of Abraham, with whom God made a covenant: "I will bless those who bless you, and the one who curses you I will curse; and in you all the families of the earth shall be blessed" (Gen. 12:3). Both Jews and Christians believe that this covenant with Abraham begins a new chapter in the history of God's interactions with humanity, a history that will one day culminate in the restoration of God's primordial blessing of all creation. They differ, of course, in the role they assign to Jesus in that culmination.

In Jesus's day, the fulfillment of God's promise to bless Abraham's family, and through this to bless all the families of the earth, was widely expected to involve God sending a savior, an anointed one, who would make the Israelites into a great nation once again, defeating their enemies and establishing the worship of the God of Israel throughout the world. It was not expected to involve what Jesus foretold to his followers: that the Messiah would "undergo great suffering, and be rejected by the elders, the chief priests, and the scribes, and be killed, and after three days rise again" (Mark 8:31). This idea of a suffering Messiah was so shocking to Jesus's own disciples that they refused to believe such a thing could happen; they expected up until the last moment that Jesus would somehow divert the course of events so as to avoid the cross and unmask his true identity as the triumphant Savior of Israel. But it was not to be. God chose the cross as the means by which to give the world, as Pope Benedict puts it, "a new horizon and a decisive direction." God embraced the cross as the place to reveal the love that God is.

*   *   *

A number of years ago I was in one of the great European cathedrals standing before a large depiction of Jesus's crucifixion with a friend. It was a dramatically realistic depiction of the death of Jesus dating from the late Middle Ages, reflecting, perhaps, a consciousness seared by war and plague and social unrest. After we had stood there for a few moments contemplating the image, she commented, "You know, I'm really not into the whole guilt thing." I knew her well enough to know that she was what we today tend to call a "none"—those who, when filling out forms that ask about religious identity, check the box marked "none." She had little religious background but seemed genuinely curious about my own somewhat obsessive interest in religion, and we sometimes discussed the nature of belief and unbelief. But we had never really talked about Jesus, much less the crucifixion. At first I was puzzled by her remark. Then it dawned on me that she thought the main reason Christians put crosses in their churches is to make people feel guilty.

Her presumption is not without a certain logic. If one thinks that God imposes death upon Jesus as divine punishment for sin—a punishment that was rightly due to *us*—in order to placate God's wrath and satisfy God's justice, then one might well suspect that Christians feel as much guilt as they do gratitude for Jesus's sacrifice. After all, it was for our sins that he was punished. If the cross reminds us of the fact that a perfectly innocent person was tortured to death for our benefit, how could this not engender a measure of guilt? Isn't this how the cross works? It keeps us in line by keeping us wracked with guilt over the way our sins drive the nails into Jesus's flesh.

The nineteenth-century philosopher Friedrich Nietzsche certainly thought so. For Nietzsche, the entire apparatus of religion was the revenge of the weakest among humanity against the strongest, intended to sap their strength through guilt. The whole notion that Jesus bore our guilt appalled Nietzsche: "The *guilt sacrifice*, and that in its most repulsive, barbaric form, the sacrifice of the *innocent man* for the sins of the guilty!" (*Anti-Christ*, 41). For Nietzsche, the fictional gods of antiquity, the gods we meet in the "Knight's Tale" who sought only their own good, were far preferable to the no-less-fictional Christian God: "there are *nobler* uses for the invention of gods than for the self-crucifixion and self-violation of man" (*Genealogy of Morals*, 2.23). The crucifixion of Jesus, conceived primarily in terms of a transfer of guilt, has the odd effect of loading that guilt back upon the one who has supposedly been freed from guilt through the sacrifice of an innocent, such that the original guilt is now amplified to the point where the human will is broken, human pride is humbled, and the powerful subject themselves to God. For Nietzsche, it is the triumph of self-imposed sickness over the life of the strong.

My friend and Nietzsche could certainly find evidence for this view within the Christian tradition. The seventeenth-century hymn writer Johann Heermann wrote, in a hymn addressed to the crucified Jesus:

> Who was the guilty? Who brought this upon
>   thee?
> Alas, my treason, Jesus, hath undone thee!
> 'Twas I, Lord Jesus, I it was denied thee;
> I crucified thee. ("Ah, Holy Jesus," 1630)

A friendly reading of this text—and likely the one intended by Heermann—might see it as expressing a metaphorical sense of corporate responsibility, something akin to John Donne's observation that "no man is an island," a recognition that we cannot stand apart from the wrongs of this world and point fingers at others. A less friendly, more suspicious reading of this text, one that agrees with Nietzsche about the life-denying character of Christianity, might see it as putting on the lips of worshipers a profession of guilt that, over time, fosters human self-crucifixion and self-violation.

Though not without a certain logic, I think it is mistaken to see the cross in terms of guilt over the punishment inflicted by God on Jesus instead of on us. While some Christians might think about the crucifixion in this way, many do not. The logic of the idea of Jesus as the recipient of divine punishment seems to presume that the dilemma that sin has created for the human race is chiefly one of divine anger: sin is bad for us because it angers God. Or perhaps God is bound by the demands of justice in such a way that, even if God were not angry because of sin, God could still not let go of the punishment that is due to us without becoming unjust. Both of these seem to be questionable presumptions.

Jesus's parable of the prodigal son (Luke 15:11–32), in which the father rushes out to meet his wayward son who is returning home after wasting his inheritance, suggests that God is not angry with the sinners; if we are to ascribe any emotion to God based on this parable, it would seem God's response to sin is sorrow and not anger. Likewise, there is no suggestion in the parable that the father cannot simply forgive his son, that he is bound by some inexorable justice to impose a penalty upon him. The parable does not trivialize sin, for the lost son's misdeeds cause him considerable suffering. But this penalty for sin is not something imposed by his father. It is rather, what I earlier, appealing to St. Augustine, described as the "coming close to nothingness" that follows upon our turning away from the source of our life and existence. What is most striking in the parable is that the father, who would be well within his rights to let his son come before him groveling—indeed, he would be well within his rights to continue to hold his son accountable for squandering what he had given him—does not even give the son an opportunity to grovel but casts aside his paternal dignity and runs out to meet his son and embrace him.

Jesus is the God who is love running out to meet us wayward wasters who have squandered the divine gift of our existence. The question is, why does this love that is God take the form of the cross when it shows itself to us?

*   *   *

If we are going to understand the death of Jesus as a revelation of divine love, and why God would choose such a means to show to us the love that God is, then we need to see how the cross of Jesus is related to the life of Jesus. Traditionally for Christians this has meant that the significance of Jesus's crucifixion is rooted in his identity as the eternal Son, the second person of the holy Trinity, the Word of God, who has taken upon himself our human nature. As the prologue to the Gospel of John puts it, "The Word became flesh and lived among us, and we have seen his glory, the glory as of a father's only son, full of grace and truth" (John 1:14). Born of Mary, becoming "flesh," Jesus is truly human; in the words of the fifth-century church council held at Chalcedon (alluding to the New Testament letter to the Hebrews), he is "like us in all things but sin." Yet even in taking upon himself a human nature, Jesus remains the eternal divine Son: in the words of the Nicene Creed, "born of the Father before all ages." Therefore, on account of his humanity, his death on the cross is truly a human death, but on account of his divinity the cross is truly the death of the immortal God in human flesh and therefore takes on cosmic redemptive significance as the defeat of death and sin.

Yet there is more that we can say about the connection between Jesus's life and death than this. After all, if all that mattered was that God became incarnate and died a human death, then it wouldn't have made any difference if Jesus had died as a child rather than as an adult. In connecting the life of Jesus to his death, we need to look not simply at the *fact* of his human life but also at the *kind* of human life he lived. John Chrysostom wrote in the late fourth century, "All that Jesus did and suffered was for our instruction" (*Matthew* 13.1). This means that it is not the mere fact of Jesus's life that shows forth the God who is love but the particular shape of the life he lives. And this same life is what leads to his death, not simply in the sense that all human life eventually ends in death but in the sense that how he lives his life will lead people to want to take that life from him. Ignacio Ellacuría, a priest and philosopher who worked on behalf of the poor in El Salvador, argued that the question "Why did Jesus die?" is inseparable from the question "Why did they kill him?"—and indeed "the 'why did they kill him' has a certain priority over the 'why did he die'" (*Essays on History, Liberation, and Salvation*, 232)—because Jesus does not merely die but is killed by powerful forces who take offense at his life. It is worth noting that Ellacuría himself, along with seven others, was killed in 1989 by government soldiers because of his advocacy for a negotiated peace in El Salvador's civil war.

So, what *does* Jesus do that leads to him being killed? Mark's Gospel tells us that Jesus begins his ministry by traveling through his native region of Galilee proclaiming, "The time is fulfilled, and the kingdom of God has come near; repent, and believe the good news" (Mark 1:15). What Jesus means by the "kingdom of God" is suggested by a few lines in the prayer that he taught his followers: "Your kingdom come. Your will be done, on earth as it is in heaven" (Matt. 6:10). Because human beings have abandoned God to live for themselves, the world has taken on dark contours that do not manifest what God wills for creation. The "kingdom of God" is a way of talking about the restoration of creation through God's will being done in this world in the same way that God's will is accomplished in heaven; it is an image of how the darkness of this world could be lifted if people would turn away from—repent of—living solely for themselves and turn back to living for the God who is love. What Jesus calls the good news is his proclamation that this is beginning to come to pass, the kingdom is drawing near. It is drawing near in the words and actions of Jesus himself.

How do Jesus's words and actions make God's kingdom present? The actions that draw the most attention initially—

his healings and other miracles—suggest that God's kingdom will be a time and place from which human suffering, whether sickness or hunger or natural disaster or even death, will be banished. The actions that most irritate the religious authorities of his time—the audacity of forgiving sins without requiring people to go through the prescriptions of the law given to Moses—suggest that the kingdom of God will be a time and place of reconciliation between God and humanity and among human beings. And his verbal teachings—whether explicit instructions like the Sermon on the Mount or allusive parables like the story of the prodigal son—sketch a picture of human life characterized by a willingness to be vulnerable and to trust in God, a renunciation of privilege and power and violence, and above all a sense of joy and surprise at the sheer goodness of God. These actions and words taken together not only describe the kingdom of God but show Jesus to be the one who makes that kingdom present to people.

At the heart of Jesus's proclamation of God's kingdom is a call to live as if God truly is love, a love that is, as the Old Testament Song of Songs puts it, "strong as death, passion fierce as the grave" (Song of Sol. 8:6). Jesus tells his followers, "do not keep striving for what you are to eat and what you are to drink, and do not keep worrying. For it is the nations of the world that strive after all these things, and your Father knows that you need them. Instead, strive for his kingdom, and these things will be given to you as well" (Luke 12:29–31). Jesus knows that "the nations of the world" live a life of striving after security, fearful of human enemies and an indifferent providence. Jesus is not, of course, opposed to people working for a living; he himself was apparently a carpenter by trade (Mark 6:3). But he is opposed to worldly striving that proceeds as if we are each in this thing for ourselves, children abandoned by God our Father to make our own way. He is opposed to any way of life that by its anxious striving and lack of trust denies the love that is God. He calls his followers to strive instead for the kingdom that is free of striving.

We might wonder: why would his proclaiming of the kingdom of God and making it present in word and action make anyone want to kill Jesus? It is worth remembering that the phrase "kingdom of God" is a political metaphor. So too is the term *messiah*, which increasingly is applied to Jesus over the course of his ministry. It is associated with ancient Israel's king David, whose reign is held up as an ideal to which later kingdoms failed to measure up. Jesus's proclamation of the drawing near of God's kingdom is heard by many as a veiled political threat: he is preparing for a kingdom that will replace the ruling political and religious authorities and restore things to the Davidic ideal. And these powerful forces are not wrong in seeing Jesus as a threat. While he has no intention of setting up an alternative kingdom as they understand it, he *is* saying that through him it is now possible to live in a new way, enlivened by the love that is God, free from worldly striving, and that living in this way will show that all worldly kingdoms are built on domination rather than vulnerability, violence rather than peace, grasping rather than trust. We might say that the words and actions of Jesus do not so much seek to tear down the walls of earthly kingdoms as to undermine their foundations so they will collapse under their own weight.

And this must not happen. It would result in chaos. If military might and religious obedience do not keep a lid on things, the passions seething just below the surface of human society will burst forth in uncontrollable fury. Better to let the Roman governor and the high priests in Jerusalem direct focused fury at Jesus. Better to take Jesus definitively out of the picture. As the high priest, Caiaphas, says to the council that controls religious affairs in Israel, "It is better for you to have one man die for the people than to have the whole nation destroyed" (John 11:50).

So the death of Jesus flows from his proclamation of God's kingdom, from the audacity of saying that in his words and actions the kingdom of God has drawn near. If Jesus were, as some people claim, a simple teacher of commonsense morality, a purveyor of the golden rule that we should do unto others as we would have them do unto us, then it would be difficult to understand why he would have been killed by powerful political and religious forces. If, however, the kingdom he makes present is the subversive kingdom of love, the kingdom that undermines all forms of human life built on power and domination, then it requires no great feat of imagination to see why those who have power, those who are in dominant positions, would have him killed. And it is understandable why he would die by crucifixion, a mode of execution that the Romans reserved for slaves and rebels, a death by public torture intended to be as painful and humiliating as possible so as to serve as a deterrent to others. We who have turned away from love and toward ourselves ensure by our striving that when the God who is love takes flesh and dwells among us, God takes crucified flesh and dwells among us as a slave and a rebel.

*   *   *

I once knew a man who asked me if Jesus *had* to die, by which he meant, could God have saved humanity in some way other than by the cross? Was God *forced* to have Jesus die on the cross, or did perhaps God *want* Jesus to die on the cross? This way of posing the question creates something of a dilemma since it seems to say either that God is not *able* to save us in some other way or that God is not *willing* to save us in some other way. If the first is the case, then it seems as if God is somehow limited or constrained, unwillingly forced by justice to have Jesus die. If the second is the case, then we seem to be in the uncomfortable position of saying that God desires that his Son undergoes one of the most painful and humiliating deaths that human ingenuity, in all its perversity, has devised. The first seems to give us a God who is limited in power; the second seems to give us a God who cannot be said to be love, at least not with a straight face. In either case, God ends up looking something like the limited and loveless gods of Chaucer's "Knight's Tale."

Though the question was sincerely posed, I think it is the wrong question to ask because it leaves us with unacceptable alternatives. Rather than ask why God wants Jesus to *die* the way he did, we should ask why God wants Jesus to *live* the way he did and why this way of life led us to want to *kill* him. God wants Jesus to live the reality of God's kingdom, to live the kindness that is at the core of the divine identity while also living as one of us, facing all of the trials and troubles that fragile human flesh must face. God wants Jesus to live this way so he can show us what life in the kingdom of God—truly human life—is all about. And not simply to show us but also to forge a path into that kingdom, to give us a way to be what God created us to be.

God wants Jesus to live this way even though God knows that such a life will get him killed. As a parent, I desire more than anything that my children know the love of God and live according to that knowledge. This means that I desire them to live lives that are free from worldly striving and control, lives of generosity and vulnerability, lives that are marked by a passion for justice and concern for the downtrodden. But I am not naive. I desire this for them knowing well that people who live such lives are often taken advantage of and have to forgo material pleasures and security. I desire this knowing that some may hate them for living such lives and see them as agents of chaos undermining the very foundations of society. I desire this knowing that some may even try to harm them, seeing them as somehow both threatening and defenseless (an irresistible combination for the human impulse to find scapegoats). But even in light of knowing all this, what I desire for them are lives rooted in God's love, not the negative effects that I foresee will likely, perhaps inevitably, accompany such lives when they are lived out in a world that has turned from love. God desires that divine love be incarnate in Jesus, even knowing that this will be too much love for a grasping, frustrated, frightened world to bear. God desires that love be incarnate, even if that love must be crucified.

In one of the odder questions that he contemplates, Thomas Aquinas asks whether Jesus should have been slaughtered and burned instead of crucified. As his imagined interlocutor puts it, "In all the sacrifices of the Old Testament that foreshadowed Christ, the beasts were slain with a sword and afterwards consumed by fire. It seems then that Christ ought not to have suffered on a cross, but rather by the sword or by fire." In answering this question, Aquinas points out, somewhat unconvincingly, that at least the cross, like a fire, involved wood. But then he makes a striking observation: "instead of material fire, there was the spiritual fire of love in Christ's burnt offering" (*Summa theologiae* 3.46.4). What Aquinas realizes is that at the heart of Jesus's sacrifice is not his death but his love. This sacrifice of love returns to God what rightly is owed to God by human beings. It is Jesus's love for the one he calls Father, and his desire that his Father's will be done in him as it is in heaven, that is offered up on the cross. The offering of the cross is simply the continuation of what he offered to God throughout his life: unconditional commitment to the cause of God's kingdom, complete openness to God and trust in the power of divine love, and a hunger and thirst for righteousness. It also tells us something about what we have made of this world that such an offering would inevitably culminate in crucifixion—an inevitability born entirely of human rejection of love.

*   *   *

Even if the crucifixion unveils for us the nature of God as love, if that were where the story ended, it would only serve to show us the tragedy of love: God is love, and to love like God will get you killed. Though this is true, it is hard to see how this could be the good news of the kingdom that Jesus came to proclaim unless one finds satisfaction in stoic resignation to suffering and death. It is hard to see how this could be the definitive manifestation in history of the joyful act of love that is the Trinity unless suffering and death were eternal and not contingent realities. But Christians do not believe this is the end of the story. Christians believe that crucified love cannot be contained in the tomb but bursts forth in that mysterious event that we call resurrection. If Jesus's crucifixion cannot be properly understood apart from the life that precedes it, it likewise cannot be understood apart from the resurrection that follows it.

The New Testament's accounts of the resurrection are somewhat varied in detail, but most include both the finding empty of Jesus's tomb by a group of his women followers and a number of appearances by the risen Jesus to various people. Paul writes of these appearances in his first letter to the Christians in the city of Corinth:

> I handed on to you as of first importance what I in turn had received: that Christ died for our sins in accordance with the scriptures, and that he was buried, and that he was raised on the third day in accordance with the scriptures, and that he appeared to Cephas [Peter], then to the twelve. Then he appeared to more than five hundred brothers and sisters at one time, most of whom are still alive, though some have died. Then he appeared to James,

> then to all the apostles. Last of all, as to someone untimely
> born, he appeared also to me. (1 Cor. 15:3–8)

The actual nature of these appearances is somewhat mysterious because the risen Jesus is one who now lives fully in God's kingdom. Some who see him do not at first recognize him. He can walk through locked doors and vanish in an instant. And yet the Gospels insist that this is not simply the "spirit" of Jesus living on after the death of his body. The same body that was crucified is now risen; the tomb where his body was laid is now empty, and he bears the marks of crucifixion. Just as the love that is God was embodied in crucified flesh, it now lives in resurrected flesh. The forces of death-dealing self-love that killed Jesus have been truly defeated by love crucified and risen.

This event of resurrection is the seed bed from which the Christian faith springs forth. The one who had died a death that seemed to show his rejection by God is now the one proclaimed as universal Lord. The experience of the risen Jesus transforms his followers from a frightened and scattered group, terrified that the fate that befell their master might befall them as well, into those who boldly proclaim that a new era has begun in which death's power is vanquished. This same experience transforms Paul from a persecutor of the nascent Jesus movement into a bearer of the good news of Jesus, who journeys to the ends of the known world. Some have argued that it is this well-attested transformation of those who claim to have encountered the risen Jesus that provides the best argument for the truth of his resurrection.

*   *   *

In Julian of Norwich's account of the vision she received of Christ suffering on the cross, she speaks of how she was looking at a physical crucifix when "suddenly I saw the red blood trickle down from under the crown [of thorns], hot and fresh, plentiful and vivid, just as it was at the time that the crown of thorns was pressed on his blessed head." She then says, "In the same vision suddenly the Trinity filled my heart full of joy. . . . The Trinity is our maker, the Trinity is our keeper, the Trinity is our everlasting lover, the Trinity is our endless joy and our bliss, by our Lord Jesus Christ and in our Lord Jesus Christ. . . . For where Jesus appears the Trinity is understood, as I see it." (*Revelations of Divine Love*, chap. 4)

It would no doubt surprise both my friend in the cathedral and Nietzsche that looking at the crucifix does not fill Julian with guilt and lead her to groveling self-castigation. Instead, it fills her with joy. Joy is precisely what Nietzsche thought Christianity drained from life and is what he sought to restore to humanity in his own *fröhliche Wissenschaft*, or "joyful science." It was in a work of this name that Nietzsche told his "parable of the madman," in which a man with a lantern burning in the middle of the day runs into the marketplace asking "Where has God gone?" and then answers his own question: "I shall tell you. We have killed him—you and I. We are his murderers. But how have we done this? How were we able to drink up the sea? Who gave us the sponge to wipe away the entire horizon? What did we do when we unchained the earth from its sun?" This killing of God, this unmooring of the human world, is seen by Nietzsche as a great liberation for the higher type of human, a calling to a kind of self-deification: "Is not the greatness of this deed too great for us? Must we not ourselves become gods simply to be worthy of it?" (*Joyful Science*, 125). God must die for joy to be born in us.

There is a sense in which Nietzsche is right. Julian's vision also connects the death of God—the death of Jesus on the cross—and the birth of joy. However, Julian sees in crucified love not the overcoming of God or the self-deification of humanity but love running forth in joy to embrace the wayward human race, journeying even as far as the place of death, and bringing humanity into the interpersonal, generative, joyful love that is the holy Trinity. In a world marked by human self-seeking, the cross is the cost of joy being restored to the world, a cost that is joyfully paid by Jesus out of love for humanity.

Christians sometimes treat the Trinity as a form of celestial mathematics that no human mind can comprehend, something that must simply be believed as a kind of loyalty test. But when Julian says that "where Jesus appears the Trinity is understood," she suggests that, while the Trinity *is* beyond our comprehension, we are not without reasons for this belief, and that Christians profess that God is Father, Son, and Holy Spirit because this threefold reality of God is shown to us in Jesus, who is the eternal Son sent by his Father in the power of the Spirit. Jesus's life of vulnerable trust, his proclamation of a kingdom free from worldly striving, his willingness to suffer the cost of his faithfulness to that kingdom, his rising from the tomb to give life and hope to his followers—all of this is the manifestation in history of the eternal joy that is Father, Son, and Spirit. Just as Jesus pours himself out in love of God and neighbor, so too the Father pours himself out in love, bringing forth the Son, and the Son in turn pours himself out in love of the Father, and from this mutual self-emptying in love the Spirit is breathed forth. The life of the kingdom that Jesus proclaims is creation's sharing in the life of the Trinity. The life of the Trinity, like life in the kingdom, is free of earthly striving. The Trinity, like the cross, is a pure self-giving in love; unlike the cross, however, it is unmarred by the suffering and violence that human sin imposes. Its only labor is the joyful labor of delight.

We might still ask what all this has to do with us. Jesus is killed and raised, and this shows us the love that is God, but how does this change our human condition of alienation from God? How does this pull us back from the edge of "almost nothingness"? How does this bring us into joy? How, we might say, does crucified love become a saving mystery in our lives? To begin to answer these questions, we must contemplate further the work of the Holy Spirit, which is the work of God's good pleasure within us, transforming us into friends of God.

Further Reading

- The Gospel of Mark. Widely regarded as the oldest of the four Gospels of the New Testament, written around AD 70, Mark's Gospel has been called "a passion narrative with a long introduction." Indeed, from the outset Mark's story is directed to the suffering and death of Jesus, a path that he walks amid conflict and misunderstanding, even by his own followers. Mark's central message is that one cannot understand what it means for Jesus to be God's anointed apart from the cross.

- Julian of Norwich, *Revelations of Divine Love.* This text, from the late fourteenth or early fifteenth century, is the oldest work in English written by a woman. It is the fruit of Julian's years of reflection on sixteen visions, most of which are centered on the crucified Jesus, that she received in her early thirties. After her visions, she spent her life trying to discern what God meant by them before finally arriving at the conclusion that "love was his meaning."

3

We are called to friendship with the risen Jesus.

The thread of friendship runs throughout the story of Jesus's life. The four Gospels introduce us to Jesus by displaying his life against a backdrop of key relationships: to Peter and Judas, both of whom in different ways will betray him in the end; to Mary Magdalene and John, who will remain faithful to him as he goes to the cross; to Mary and Martha of Bethany and to their brother Lazarus, at whose grave Jesus will weep; and to a host of named and unnamed sinners and outcasts whom Jesus eats with and preaches to, heals and forgives. We see Jesus celebrating at a wedding that is apparently so raucous that they run out of wine (John 2:1-11). We see him befriending Zacchaeus the tax collector and even inviting himself to Zacchaeus's house (Luke 19:1-10). We see Jesus so delighting in sharing food and drink with people that he offends those whose image of a holy man runs in a more ascetic vein, who accuse him of being a glutton and a drunk (Matt. 11:18-19). Wherever Jesus goes, he invites people into friendship with him.

If Jesus is truly risen from the dead, then friendship with him is still possible. The claim of Christians is not that Jesus was a figure of the past who did some good things and taught some valuable lessons from which we can still learn today. When Pope Benedict speaks of the heart of Christianity being an encounter with a person, he is not thinking of how we might "encounter" Genghis Khan or Thomas Jefferson in the pages of a history text. He means rather that Jesus still lives—indeed, is more truly alive than we are—and continues to form new bonds of friendship with people, bonds of friendship in which we come to share in his life. This bond of friendship is the Holy Spirit, whose effect in our lives is what we call "grace."

*   *   *

The account in the Gospel of John of Jesus's Last Supper with his followers is considerably longer than what we find in the other three Gospels, extending over five chapters. Relatively little is said of the meal itself; most of the account is taken up with Jesus teaching his followers and praying for them to his Father. In the course of teaching them he says, "I do not call you servants any longer, because a servant does not know what his master is doing; but I have called you friends, because I have made known to you everything that I have heard from my Father" (John 15:15). He also promises that "the Advocate, the Holy Spirit, whom the Father will send in my name, will teach you everything, and remind you of all that I have said to you" (John 14:26). This "Advocate" or "Helper" or "Comforter"—the Greek word used is *paraklētos*, which indicates someone called to one's side to give aid, perhaps in a court of law—sustains in Jesus's followers the divine knowledge that he has given them, the knowledge that makes possible friendship with him. In John's account of Jesus's resurrection, Jesus breathes on his disciples and says, "Receive the Holy Spirit" (John 20:22), for it is through this Spirit that ongoing friendship with the risen Jesus is possible, not just for the disciples of his day but for all Christians down through history.

The giving of the Spirit, the Comforter, is recounted in more dramatic fashion in the Acts of the Apostles. Fifty days after Jesus's resurrection the Spirit descends on the gathered disciples with "a sound like the rush of a violent wind" and appears among them in "divided tongues, as of fire" (Acts 2:2–3). But whether like a breath or a rushing wind and flame, the Holy Spirit is depicted as the risen Jesus's gift to his friends, by which they continue to share in his crucified love even when he is no longer present to them in an ordinary, bodily way. This Spirit has not, however, been previously absent from the story of Jesus. It is through an act of the Spirit that Jesus is conceived in the womb of the Virgin Mary; it is the Spirit who descends upon Jesus in his baptism; it is the Spirit who fills Jesus as he inaugurates his ministry at the synagogue in Nazareth. In some ancient manuscripts, we find in the Gospel of Luke's version of the Lord's Prayer, immediately after the request "your kingdom come," the phrase, "Your Holy Spirit come upon us and cleanse us." This suggests that some early Christians associated the arrival of God's kingdom with the gift of the Holy Spirit. The Spirit makes present in us the reign of God that Jesus himself made present in his bodily words and actions.

Christians traditionally see the Holy Spirit manifested even earlier in Scripture, as the breath or wind of God that moved over the waters of chaos in the creation story (the Hebrew word *rûah*, like the Greek *pneuma*, can mean either "spirit" or "breath" or "wind"). The Spirit is sometimes associated with the wisdom of God, which is personified in the Old Testament and deuterocanonical books of the Bible as a beautiful woman who draws people to God:

> while remaining in herself,
>> she renews all things;
> in every generation she passes into holy souls
> and makes them friends of God, and prophets.
>> (Wisd. of Sol. 7:27).

The prophets of the Old Testament are often said to speak by the Spirit of God. But what is striking in this description of Lady Wisdom is the claim that she makes holy souls into friends of God. What Jesus teaches at the Last Supper is anticipated by Solomon: the work of the Spirit of wisdom is not to make us slaves or servants of God but friends. Indeed, the idea of friendship with God can be discerned even in the story of creation, in which the first humans are depicted as enjoying an intimate companionship with God, a companionship that is broken when they sin and hide from his gaze in shame.

*   *   *

I sometimes tell students that the most important moral decisions they have made and will make are those regarding who their friends will be. They seem to find this mildly shocking since they associate having friends with being happy, not with being good. What they do not seem to realize is that happiness is at the heart of morality; to be a good person is to be a happy person, provided that happiness is properly understood. Friendship is likewise at the heart of morality, or at least some friendships are.

What do we mean by *friendship*? The Greek philosopher Aristotle, who lived in the fourth century before Christ, developed an account of friendship that proved to be influential among Christians like Thomas Aquinas. According to Aristotle, friendship is a kind of mutually recognized benevolence (*Nicomachean Ethics* 8.2 1156ª). This mutual well-wishing draws people into an intimate sharing of goods so that Aristotle says that "there is nothing so characteristic of friends as living together" (8.5 1157ᵇ). We can think in terms of three sorts of friendship: friendships we have because they suit our needs, friendships we have because they give us pleasure, and friendships we have because of an "excellence" of character (the Greek word *aretē*, which is often translated as "virtue") that we see in the other person (8.3 1156ª⁻ᵇ). A person of good character "delights in excellent actions and is vexed at vicious ones" just as a musically skilled person "enjoys beautiful tunes but is pained at bad ones" (9.3 1170ª). People who excel at being human (which is what Aristotle means by moral virtue) admire such excellence in others and are drawn to them. They derive enjoyment from friendship with those who are good, which is different from the enjoyment one derives from friendship with those who are amusing or pretty or otherwise pleasant, and this enjoyment is what we properly call happiness. It is this friendship among the good that for Aristotle is the truest and most enduring form of friendship. In such friendship, one desires the good of the other as much as one desires one's own good, for one's friend is "another self" (9.4 1166[a]).

But Aristotle thinks that friendship among the good is not simply a matter of mutual admiration of one another's goodness, but it is also a means by which people become better: "a certain training in excellence arises also from the company of the good" (9.3 1170[a]). Just as someone who has achieved some level of musical facility becomes a better musician by playing with those who are skilled in the art of music, so too a person who desires to be a good person becomes a better person through friendship with those who are good. As we strive to be like our friends by engaging in the activity of being good, we experience the joy of human existence at full stretch, just as the musician who is pressed to the limits of her ability by those with whom she plays knows best the joys of musicianship. This is why we want to play in the best ensemble we can, why we want to play sports with those who are more skilled than we are, or why we engage in conversation with those who know more than we do. Those who think they show their excellence by only performing with less-skilled musicians or only playing sports with lesser athletes or only arguing with people who are uninformed or mentally clumsy do not know the difference between being excellent and showing off. And they will never achieve true excellence because they will never be pushed and drawn by those more skilled than themselves. Indeed, what skill they possess will over time degrade.

Likewise, it is possible to befriend morally corrupt people with the idea that this will make us feel superior. There can be a perverse attraction exerted on us by those who consistently make poor life choices, because they can both make us feel needed and make us feel better about our own life choices. But as with the degradation of musical or athletic or intellectual skills, so too moral excellence—our skill at being human—can be degraded by the company we keep. St. Paul seems to agree with Aristotle when he writes in his first letter to the Corinthians, "Bad company ruins good morals" (1 Cor. 15:33). Likewise. Augustine, in a well-known section of his *Confessions*, recounts what to some might seem to be a harmless childhood misadventure of stealing pears with friends from a neighbor's tree, but which Augustine depicts in somber and anguished tones that evoke the primal fall of humanity into sin. He believes that friendship is "a nest of love and gentleness because of the unity it brings about between many souls" (*Confessions* 2.5.10), yet when he thinks of how he and his friends goaded each other on in their actions, he writes, "Alone I would not have committed that crime, in which my pleasure lay not in what I was stealing but in the act of theft. But had I been alone, it would have given me absolutely no pleasure, nor would I have committed it. Friendship can be a dangerous enemy, a seduction of the mind lying beyond the reach of investigation" (2.9.17). For Aristotle, Paul, and Augustine, choosing your friends is one of the most important, and perilous, moral choices you make.

There is an undeniable affinity between Aristotle's account of friendship and the Christian one. Aristotle even writes that the morally good person "does many acts for the sake of his friends and his country, and if necessary dies for them" (*Nicomachean Ethics* 9.8 1169ᵃ), which is reminiscent of Jesus's words, "No one has greater love than this, to lay down one's life for one's friends" (John 15:13). And yet there are elements in the Christian account of friendship with God that do not fit easily into Aristotle's framework. For example, though Paul and Augustine seem to agree with Aristotle on the corrupting effect of friendship with those of bad character, Jesus is notorious for hanging out with the most disreputable sorts of people, seemingly without concern that their vices will rub off on him. His defense—"Those who are well have no need of a physician, but those who are sick" (Mark 2:17)—seems unconcerned with the possibility of contagion.

Moreover, Aristotle is dismissive of the notion of divine-human friendship: "When one party is removed to a great distance, as God is, the possibility of friendship ceases" (*Nicomachean Ethics* 8.7 1159ᵃ). Perhaps the kind of deity he has in mind is one of the capricious gods or the seemingly indifferent providence that we meet in "The Knight's Tale." But as we have seen, the Old Testament speaks of how Wisdom makes people into friends of God and depicts God entering into a relationship of love with human beings, as when the book of Exodus says that "the LORD used to speak to Moses face to face, as one speaks to a friend" (Exod. 33:11). Commenting on the story of Moses, the fourth-century theologian Gregory of Nyssa writes, "We regard falling from God's friendship as the only thing dreadful, and we consider becoming God's friend the only thing worth of honor and desire" (*Life of Moses* 320). Jesus suggests that in entering into friendship with him, one enters into friendship with God. In John's Gospel, he says, "Those who love me will keep my word, and my Father will love them, and we will come to them and make our home with them" (John 14:23). If, as Aristotle puts it, it is characteristic of friends to live together, then Jesus's promise that he and his Father will make a home with those who are drawn into mutual love with him and the Father is a promise of divine friendship. So, while much can be learned from Aristotle's reflections on friendship, Christian faith seems to shift friendship onto a different footing, one that allows us to believe that God befriends us even when our failings should make us God's enemies. As Paul puts it in his letter to the Christians of Rome, "God proves his love for us in that while we still were sinners Christ died for us. . . . [W]hile we were enemies, we were reconciled to God through the death of his Son" (Rom. 5:8, 10).

*   *   *

Aristotle thought that what was most natural for friends was that they live together, sharing a common life, because he thought that friends should as much as possible always be bearing each other in mind, and "this will be realized in their living together and sharing in discussion and thought; for this is what living together would seem to mean in the case of man, and not, as in the case of cattle, feeding in the same place" (*Nicomachean Ethics* 9.9 1170^b). In other words, friendship entails conversation. And if we are called to friendship with God through the risen Jesus, then we are called to a life of conversation with God. Which is another way of saying that we are called to pray.

Prayer is difficult. It is difficult for a variety of reasons: it can be boring; it can be frightening; it can be frustrating; it can be embarrassing; it can be plagued by distractions. Perhaps most of all, it is peculiar to engage in conversation, to share discussion and thought, with someone you cannot see (though perhaps not as strange for us as it was for our ancestors) and who does not respond in ordinary human words. People often feel that their attempts at prayer are met with a deafening silence and degenerate into an endless series of unanswered requests.

Thérèse of Lisieux, the nineteenth-century French Carmelite nun known among Catholics as "the Little Flower," who died of tuberculosis at age twenty-four, wrote, "For me, prayer is an impulse of the heart, it is a simple glance turned toward heaven, it is a cry of recognition and love in the midst of trial as well as joy; finally, it is something great, supernatural, which expands my soul and unites me to Jesus" (*Story of a Soul*, chap. 11). This description of prayer gets at something very primal about prayer, certain things that seem to be true about prayer in its many varied forms, and it is unblinking in recognizing the difficulties of prayer.

First, it describes prayer as "an impulse of the heart." The French word Thérèse uses—*élan*—can also mean a yearning or aspiration. For Thérèse, to want to pray *is* to pray. This is an insight that grows from her own experience. In the last months of her life, when she was sick and dying and needed God most, she experienced great difficulty with prayer, feeling that God was absent and heaven was closed to her. To her physical suffering was added terrible spiritual suffering, but she never lost her *desire* to pray; at the very least, she *wanted* to want to pray, wanted to sustain her conversation with God. Despite her youth, she was wise enough to know that the yearning of her heart for prayer was itself a prayer, indeed, the most basic form of prayer possible.

Second, Thérèse's description of prayer does not require any complex techniques. When you're dying, you can't concern yourself too much with breathing exercises or guided imagery or elaborate devotions or carefully formed phrases, as useful as these might seem in other contexts. All it takes, she says, is "a simple glance turned toward heaven." Given her own physical and spiritual suffering, this was perhaps all she could manage. But is it really all that different for the rest of us? We too have our doubts and difficulties. We too have our anxieties and troubles. Sometimes all we can muster is a simple glance turned toward heaven, reminding ourselves that there is a God or that we want there to be a God, or that we want to want there to be a God and that we want to see God and to know that God sees us, our troubles, and our joys.

Third, Thérèse says that prayer is something "supernatural." She doesn't mean by this that it is spooky or involves extraordinary occurrences. She means simply that it comes to us from God and that even our bare impulse to pray, our desire to want to pray, is a divine gift that we could never earn or deserve. It is something that we cannot live without, and it is entirely dependent on God's love for us. This might seem a frightening thought. After all, we don't like being dependent on others for things that are vitally important to us. We like to be able to do for ourselves those things that are really important so we can have them within our control. Even with friends, we want to take the lead in conversation. We forget that God's love for us is far more dependable than anything we could do for ourselves because God *is* love. To recognize prayer as something we cannot live without and yet something that can only be received as a gift from God is to surrender control in a radical way.

Fourth, Thérèse says that the supernatural reality of prayer "expands" the soul. The French word she uses is *dilate*, which suggests that just as the pupil of the eye expands to let in more light, so too the soul expands to let in the light of God that comes to us in prayer. To let prayer dilate the soul is to have our hearts expanded, to make them more like God's heart. That means that the chief effect of prayer, as Thérèse understands it, is not to bend God's will to ours but rather to have our wills conformed to God, to begin to love as God loves, to let our souls contain all that God's love contains. Thomas Aquinas calls prayer "the interpreter of desire" (*Summa theologiae* 2-2.83.9). When we pray, particularly when we ask God to give us those things that we deeply desire, we suddenly see those desires in the light of God, their nobility or pettiness revealed. And when we let prayer interpret our desire, we cast aside the agenda of our own desires to let God's desires guide us, for God's desire is more deeply for our happiness than our own desires could ever be.

Thérèse knows that having our finite souls expanded by the infinite love of God is an experience both joyous and painful.

She interprets her feelings of emptiness and abandonment by God as her having taken into her own heart, as a part of God's love, the experience of all those who feel the world to be empty of God, those who doubt, all those who place their faith in things like wealth or fame or technology to fill the gap left by the God whom they have tried to expel from their souls. All the unbelief of the modern world, she says, becomes her own experience because God is expanding, dilating, stretching her heart so that she can know and love the atheist, the agnostic, the unbeliever in something like the way God knows and loves them. Prayer, Thérèse knows, is a dangerous business. Because it draws us into the reality of God, it also draws us into the pain and suffering of the world that God loves and, if we let it, stretches and even tears our souls so we can love the world in the way that God does.

And in doing this, it unites our souls to Jesus, the one in whom God knows intimately how our world struggles and suffers. Jesus prays as he weeps at the tomb of his friend Lazarus; he prays as he weeps for himself in the Garden of Gethsemane; he prays as he hangs in agony on the cross. Indeed, his whole life is a prayer because it is the expression in time of the eternal conversation of love that is the life of God as Father, Son, and Holy Spirit. In the stillness of eternity, God the Father speaks the Son as his Word, and as the Son responds in love, the Spirit is breathed forth. Through friendship with Jesus in the Spirit, we have become part of that eternal dialogue of love. Even when we feel that we hear no answer, our souls expand in prayer to include all that the heart of Jesus loves, all that God loves, the entire world in its joys and sorrows, and in this dilation of our soul we know the cross and resurrection of Jesus, the mystery of crucified love.

*   *   *

Aristotle's remark that human friendship is not, as it is with the bovine companionship of cattle, a matter of feeding in the same place, should not make us underestimate the role of food and drink in the common life of friends. The ancient *symposium*—what we might think of as a philosophical dinner party with lots of wine—was often the context for the sharing in thought and discussion of which Aristotle speaks. We can all recognize the activity of *dining*, as opposed to simply *feeding*, as a distinctively human activity, one marked not only by consumption but also by conversation. Many today lament the perceived loss of the family dinner table marked by a lively exchange in which the events of the day were shared and discussed, where family bonds were formed and family identity passed on. Even if we are looking back through a haze of nostalgia (I am pretty sure that family meals were not always so idyllic, nor am I convinced that they have entirely vanished), there is something about the ideal of the shared meal marked by that most human of things, linguistic communication, that suggests dining together is at the heart of human friendship and flourishing.

Indeed, dining plays a significant role in the life of Jesus as a means by which he forges ties with people. He often teaches in the context of meals, and, as mentioned, a significant portion of John's Gospel takes the form of a lengthy after-dinner speech. In the other Gospels, Jesus speaks of God's kingdom in terms of a banquet (Matt. 22:2; 25:10) and anticipates dining in the kingdom through miracles that bring about an abundance of food (Mark 6:35-43; 8:1-9) as well as by dining with sinners and others who would normally be excluded from table fellowship, especially with a holy man like Jesus (Mark 2:13-17). If friendship with Jesus constitutes friendship with God, then by inviting sinners to sit with him and dine, Jesus seeks to reconcile them with God, no matter how scandalous that practice might be. Moreover, he encourages his friends to continue for themselves his own practice of scandalous dining: "When you give a luncheon or a dinner, do not invite your friends or your brothers or your relatives or rich neighbors, in case they may invite you in return, and you would be repaid. But when you give a banquet, invite the poor, the crippled, the lame, and the blind. And you will be blessed, because they cannot repay you, for you will be repaid at the resurrection of the righteous" (Luke 14:12-14). The imperative of becoming a friend of Jesus overrides all considerations of prudence or propriety or calculation of advantage. In his dining with friends, as in all other things, Jesus lives his life with abandon and complete trust in God. His meals are crucified love in the form of food and drink.

This is true above all of the last meal he eats with his inner circle of followers. Here the boundaries of the table are more tightly drawn, but the meaning of meal is the same scandalous love that Jesus shows to sinners. At that last supper, Jesus again makes reference to God's kingdom (Luke 22:16) but adds something new: he points toward his impending death, and, taking bread and giving thanks, he breaks it and gives it to them with the words, "This is my body, which is given for you. Do this in remembrance of me" (Luke 22:19). Then, after they have eaten together, he takes a cup of wine and shares it with them, saying, "This cup that is poured out for you is the new covenant in my blood" (Luke 22:20). In speaking of the covenant, Jesus evokes the bond of friendship that God forged with Abraham and his descendants: Moses and David and Solomon and all the prophets. But now this bond is sealed not with the sacrifice of animals, as had previously been the case, but with Jesus's own life, his crucified love given and poured out for them. In this meal, God's friendship with humanity through Jesus is established in a definitive and irrevocable way.

In Luke's Gospel, after Jesus is crucified and the women find Jesus's empty tomb and rumors begin to spread of strange happenings in Jerusalem, two of his followers fleeing the city meet a stranger on the road. They share with him the story of all that had happened concerning Jesus in the previous few days, concluding, "We had hoped that he was the one to redeem Israel" (Luke 24:21). We *had* hoped: this word *hope*, grammatically stranded in the past, exiled from its native land, the future, points to their dreams of the kingdom now shattered on the cross. In response to their disappointment and perplexity, the stranger begins to teach them how all of these things had been foretold in the sacred writings of the Israelites. Moved by his words, they urge the stranger to continue walking with them until they come to a village called Emmaus, where they stop for the night. As they sit down to share a meal, the stranger takes bread and, giving thanks, breaks it and gives it to them. Suddenly they recognize the stranger as Jesus, the crucified and risen one, who then immediately vanishes from their sight. They say to each other, "Were not our hearts burning within us while he was talking to us on the road?" (Luke 24:32). Immediately they return to Jerusalem, to the city from which they had been fleeing, to bring the good news that Jesus still lives, still breaks bread with them in friendship, still converses and speaks and dines with them.

To this day, Christians still dine with Jesus in the sacrificial meal of the Eucharist (a Greek word that means "thanksgiving"), also called the Lord's Supper or the Mass. As with the disciples at Emmaus, the risen Jesus still opens up the Scriptures to his friends and shares a meal with them in which he gives himself to them in love as food and drink. Thomas Aquinas appeals to Aristotle's claim that there is nothing so characteristic of friends as living together in support of his belief that Christ's presence in the bread and wine of the Eucharist is a bodily, and not merely symbolic, presence (*Summa theologiae* 3.75.1). The Eucharist is the medium in which ongoing friendship with Jesus is lived out. The gathering of all time into this sacramental celebration is expressed in a liturgical text that Aquinas penned for the feast of *Corpus Christi*, which is celebrated in honor of the Eucharist:

> O sacred banquet!
> in which Christ is received,
> the memory of his passion is renewed,
> the mind is filled with grace,
> and a pledge of future glory to us is given.
> Alleluia.

In this sacred banquet, past, present, and future come together as Christians gather joyfully to recall what the theologian Johann Baptist Metz has called the "dangerous memory" of Jesus. They gather to know, present now through sacred signs, the real presence of his crucified love. They gather to look forward to feasting with him in the kingdom of peace, crushed dreams resurrected. In this meal, Jesus continues to live with his friends in the most intimate way possible.

Julian of Norwich presses this intimacy even further, shifting the metaphor from friendship to parenthood. Employing a startling image, she compares Jesus in the Eucharist to a nursing mother: "the mother may give her child her milk to suck, but our precious Mother Jesus, he may feed us with himself, and does so with great courtesy and great tenderness with the blessed sacrament that is the precious food of true life" (*Revelations of Divine Love*, chap. 60). For Julian, Jesus is our true mother because he gives himself to us as the food of the kingdom, to sustain us on the journey to eternity. In the Eucharist, the body and blood of Jesus are truly present, not as mere objects for consumption, but as the active handing over of himself to us in love. Jesus's words in John's Gospel—"unless you eat the flesh of the Son of Man and drink his blood, you have no life in you" (John 6:53)—point us toward a primal act of human connection in which life is sustained through the gift of one's own bodily substance.

*   *   *

The Eastern Christian tradition especially emphasizes the role of the Holy Spirit in bringing about Christ's presence in the Eucharist. In the liturgy of St. Basil, which dates from the fourth century, the priest prays:

> We pray to you and call upon you, O Holy of Holies, that by the favor of your goodness, your Holy Spirit may come upon us and upon the gifts here presented, to bless, sanctify, and make this bread to be the precious body of our Lord and God and Savior Jesus Christ, and this cup to be the precious blood of our Lord and God and Savior Jesus Christ, shed for the life and salvation of the world; and unite us all to one another who become partakers of the one bread and the cup in the communion of the one Holy Spirit.

This prayer is not a magical incantation to make Jesus present but a plea for intimate friendship with the risen Jesus, which is the source and goal of the Eucharist—something that we cannot initiate or sustain on our own but depends entirely on "the favor of your goodness." It is the work of God through the Holy Spirit. Just as the Spirit is the love born of the mutual love of Father and Son, so too the Spirit is the bond of friendship between Christians and God, and of Christians with each other.

To put it in a different way, the friendship that Jesus offers to his disciples is not something they have earned. He says to them in John's Gospel, "You did not choose me but I chose you" (John 15:16). In all of the Gospels, Jesus routinely is the initiator of relationships with people, calling them away from their ordinary lives and into friendship with him. The ongoing work of the Spirit is to be the initiator of friendship with God through Jesus. Paul writes, "God's love has been poured into our hearts through the Holy Spirit that has been given to us" (Rom. 5:5). This Spirit becomes the medium through which we can speak even to the God who infinitely transcends the capacities of our language: "the Spirit helps us in our weakness; for we do not know how to pray as we ought, but that very Spirit intercedes with sighs too deep for words" (Rom. 8:26). Augustine comments on this passage, "The Spirit moves the saints to plead with sighs too deep for words by inspiring them with a desire for the great and as yet unknown reality that we look forward to with patience" (Epistle 130, 15.28). The Spirit begins and sustains the conversation that is indispensable to friendship with God, a friendship that will be fulfilled in an as-yet-unimaginable heavenly glory.

The way Christians typically talk about this work of the Spirit is the term *grace*, which is how we translated the Greek word *charis*, which means "gift." Paul writes to the Christians at Ephesus, "By grace you have been saved through faith, and this is not your own doing; it is the gift of God" (Eph. 2:8). The gift-like character of God's friendship with us helps us understand why Jesus was so unconcerned about the perils of befriending sinners and outcasts, so unconcerned about the "contagion" of sin. The love that is God is present so perfectly, so abundantly, in the person of Jesus that his goodness cannot be diminished by contact with fallible and failed human beings. Because God's love is not drawn to our goodness but creates our goodness, because it is active and not reactive, the Spirit can transform God's enemies into God's friends.

We speak of God's grace both in reference to God's kindness itself—God's active benevolence toward us—and in reference to the transformation that God's kindness creates in us. At times, we may wish to emphasize grace as God's kindness itself, to focus on God's initiative in our lives. At other times, we may wish to emphasize the transformation that grace brings about in us, to reflect on our response to God's grace: how the work of God in us becomes our own work as we embrace the gift of God's friendship. As with any friendship, our friendship with the risen Jesus ought to deepen over time, and as it grows in depth we ought to find ourselves changed by that friendship. We should expect that we will grow in what Christians often call the "gifts of the Spirit": wisdom, understanding, counsel, courage, knowledge, reverence, and a sense of awe at God's greatness (see Isa. 11:1–2). At the same time, we can never forget that friendship with God is itself a gift and that even its growth over time is the work of the God who is love.

*   *   *

In writing his *Confessions*, Augustine of Hippo is not only pioneering the genre of memoir but is developing a theology of the working of God's grace in human lives. One might even say that he has to invent the genre because of his conviction that grace typically works in subtle, hidden ways that become apparent to us only retrospectively when our past has been gathered together into memory. He tells the story of his first thirty years as a time of seemingly aimless wandering, driven by his appetites and ambitions, but also secretly driven by the Holy Spirit, leading him ultimately to Christian baptism and friendship with the risen Jesus. This twisting path of increasing agitation appears to reach a climax in the scene of the emotionally tormented Augustine in a garden, taking up a book of Paul's letters and reading a seemingly random passage (Rom. 13:13-14), upon which "all the shadows of doubt were dispelled" (8.12.29). But Augustine is clear that, despite appearances, this sudden reversal is not a unique moment when grace begins to work but is rather a moment when grace's ongoing work becomes clearly manifest. And though he receives enough light to move forward, he also knows that this is not the end of the story of grace's work in him but rather a moment he will only understand fully when God's final judgment on the world is passed.

Throughout *Confessions*, Augustine stresses his absolute dependence on God's grace. As he tells his life's story, he underscores his inability to enter into friendship with God by his own power. He sees friendship with God, as it were, shining in the distance, but he cannot will himself to move toward it, held as he is by attachment to other things, not least of which is his life of worldly striving. His will is conflicted and pulled toward different and opposing loves, inducing a kind of moral paralysis. He writes, "The one necessary condition [for moving toward God], which meant not only going but at once arriving, was to have the will to go—provided only that the will was strong and unqualified, not the turning and twisting first this way, then that, of a will half-wounded, struggling with one part rising up and the other part falling down" (8.8.20). The wounded will cannot initiate any movement toward God but must await God's befriending. Augustine prays to God, "Grant what you command and command what you will" (10.19.40). For those who have been befriended by God, the will is joined to God in love and purified of other attachments, making it possible to embrace and embody Christ's crucified love.

Friendship plays a prominent role in Augustine's story of his life. Like Jesus in the Gospels, Augustine appears in *Confessions* surrounded by friends. We saw earlier how the friends of his youth led him astray. Other friends have a more positive effect on his character. But even those friendships that do not have a direct corrupting effect on him are not unmarked by shadow. Augustine writes movingly of the death of a friend with whom he had forged a close relationship while a young man: "My eyes looked for him everywhere, and he was not there. I hated everything because they did not have him. . . . I had become to myself a vast problem. . . . I boiled with anger, sighed, wept, and was at my wit's end. I found no calmness, no capacity for deliberation. I carried my lacerated and bloody soul when it was unwilling to be carried by me. I found no place where I could put it down" (4.4.9; 4.7.12).

The lesson Augustine seems to derive from this is that "misery is the state of every soul overcome by friendship with mortal things and lacerated when they are lost" (*Confessions* 4.6.11). When we expect the passing things of this world to bear the full weight of our love, they collapse under that weight, their own structural flaws revealed in their inability to bear that weight. Even the best of those things we love are inevitably swept away by time, and, when they pass, our love tumbles with them into their abyss. Is the answer to this misery a stoic apathy in which we do not invest ourselves in friendships so as to avoid emotional upheaval when they end, as they inevitably do?

This is not Augustine's conclusion. He continues to invest himself in friendships—indeed, Augustine's entire life and work as a bishop and writer unfolds within a network of friends (and not a few enemies)—but he now sees those friendships transformed by his friendship with God. They are not replaced by friendship with God, but they no longer need to bear the full weight of Augustine's love. They can be borne up by the love of God, the love that has been poured into our hearts through the gift of the Holy Spirit.

When Augustine's mother, Monica, dies shortly after his baptism, he describes the grief that befalls him in ways similar to his grief at his young friend's death: "my soul was wounded, and my life as it were torn to pieces, since my life and hers had become a single thing" (*Confessions* 9.12.30). He worries that now that he is a Christian such grief is inappropriate, an implicit denial of Christ's victory over death. "I was reproaching the softness of my feelings and was holding back the torrent of sadness" (9.12.31). But Augustine comes to realize that because death, even the death of a holy woman like Monica, is a relic of sin, the fruit of our ancient abandonment of God and the quest to exist in ourselves, grief is an appropriate response to human mortality. But now we weep before God, the friend who desires nothing more than to comfort us and heal the wounds that sin has inflicted on our existence. "I let flow the tears which I had held back so that they ran as freely as they wished . . . because it was your ears that were there" (9.12.33). Friendship with God does not remove grief from human life but makes it possible to grieve with hope for the kingdom where God will wipe away every tear.

One reason why grief coexists with friendship with God is that we are, to use an image beloved by Augustine, still on pilgrimage to the kingdom. Though the community of God's friends is established in eternity, it simultaneously journeys through history, deprived of any god's-eye perspective on that history, subject to regret regarding the past and dread regarding the future, living in a present moment that is stretched out between guilt and anxiety like a torture victim on the rack. Augustine writes, "You are my eternal Father, but I am scattered in times whose order I do not understand. The storms of incoherent events tear to pieces my thoughts, the inmost entrails of my soul, until that day when, purified and molten by the fire of your love, I flow together to merge into you" (*Confessions* 11.29.39).

To become God's friend is to step out in hope into an eternal moment, to be freed from regret and guilt, dread and anxiety, to gain some brief glimpse of our lives as God knows them. The act of gathering the past into memory, as Augustine does in his *Confessions*, is a dim anticipation of the gathering of souls into God's kingdom, where the truth of our lives will be revealed to us. Events that seem random, even chaotic, when viewed from within the flux of history, begin to form an intelligible pattern when viewed retrospectively from within the ambit of God's friendship. But while we still journey, this task of remembering is never complete. As life proceeds, as we grow in God's friendship, we need constantly to re-narrate that pattern, regather our past into memory, with any final telling of the story awaiting the full arrival of God's kingdom.

*   *   *

In Matthew's Gospel, just before the plot to kill Jesus is set into motion, he tells a parable about the final judgment, which will usher in the kingdom in its fullness. He depicts the human race being divided into two groups before their judge. One group will be told that they have given Jesus food when he was hungry and drink when he was thirsty, have welcomed him when he was a stranger and clothed him when he was naked, have visited him when he was imprisoned and tended him when he was sick, and these will be ushered into eternal life. The other group will be told that they have not given Jesus food when he was hungry or drink when he was thirsty, have not welcomed him when he was a stranger or clothed him when he was naked, have not visited him when he was imprisoned or tended him when he was sick, and these will be ushered into eternal fire. Both groups will express surprise at their fates. Both groups will ask when it was that they did these things or failed to do them. And the judge will reply that what they did or failed to do "to the least of these" they did or failed to do to him (Matt. 25:31–46).

This parable suggests it is only in retrospect, at the point of final judgment, that we will fully understand the meaning of our lives and the significance of our actions. It is only in retrospect that we will clearly see those moments when we have been befriended by Jesus in the distressing disguise of the poor and needy. It also suggests that somehow friendship with the risen Jesus is inseparable from friendship with our fellow human beings. In showing benevolent kindness to those who are suffering, in pouring ourselves out for them in crucified love, we are able to make the return of love to God that is essential to true friendship.

Further Reading

-   The Gospel of John. If Mark's Gospel is a passion narrative with a long introduction, John's might be thought of as the life of Jesus seen through the lens of the resurrection. In the last of the New Testament Gospels to be written, around AD 100, John presents us with significant teachings by Jesus concerning the union with God in love that is at the heart of Christianity.

-   Augustine, *Confessions*. Not simply a monument of Western culture, this memoir couched in the form of a prayer (or perhaps prayer couched in the form of a memoir) invites us into Augustine's search for God amid the sometimes-turbulent events of his life and concludes with reflections on the nature of time, memory, and creation.

4

We cannot love God if we do not love each other.

In the Gospel of John's account of the Last Supper, during his long after-dinner speech, Jesus says to his disciples, "This is my commandment, that you love one another as I have loved you" (John 15:12). This commandment is echoed by Paul in his letter to the Christians of Rome: "Owe no one anything, except to love one another; for the one who loves another has fulfilled the law" (Rom. 13:8). In both cases, love is presented as a commandment, an obligation, a debt. This runs counter to how we normally think about love. We treat laws as something external to us that we must consciously choose to obey or not, whereas love is something that we fall into, welling up from within us and yet somehow beyond our control. Arcita and Palamon do not choose to love Emily; it just happens—they are swept up and swept away. Even with the love of friendship, we are drawn to some people and not to others, whether because of their usefulness or their pleasantness or their goodness.

Though we might be forced to associate with those we find unappealing, no one can command us to be their friend.

Yet Jesus makes love an imperative—not simply love of God but love of other human beings. The first letter of John, which proclaims so boldly that God is love, likewise states the imperative of love in the strongest possible terms. "We know that we have passed from death to life because we love one another. Whoever does not love abides in death" (1 John 3:14). You cannot be friends with God, you cannot share the life of the risen Jesus, if you do not love other people. To claim to love God without engaging in the difficult task of loving those whom I encounter in my everyday life is to engage in a deadly, deceptive fantasy; I am lying to others and to myself. Again, the first letter of John says, "Those who say, 'I love God,' and hate their brothers or sisters, are liars; for those who do not love a brother or sister whom they have seen, cannot love God whom they have not seen" (1 John 4:20). I might think it is easier to love God, whom I imagine vaguely as something somewhere that is everything good and lovable, than it is to love my grimy and annoying neighbor, who is so insistently *there*, in my face, making demands. But that is because the god I claim to love is a fantasy of my own creation, not the grimy and annoying God who *is* there, on the cross, making demands. I cannot love *that* God without loving my neighbor because that God has become my neighbor.

*   *   *

Catherine of Siena accepts on faith the connection Jesus makes between love of God and love of neighbor. But, being a person of considerable intelligence who desires ever-deeper friendship with God, she seeks to glimpse *why* there is such a connection. Why should love shown to "the least of these" count as love shown to Jesus? Why should friendship with God be tied to friendship with other people? In letters, prayers, and her own account of her personal revelations from God, Catherine articulates a theology uniting love of God and love of neighbor.

If we are called by Jesus to be friends of God, then what it means to be such a friend must bear some resemblance to what friendship is among human beings. One of the things we saw in Aristotle's account of friendship is that true friendship must be mutual; both parties in the friendship must be aware of the friendship and derive benefit from it. Friendship without mutuality is called stalking (think of Arcita and Palamon's initial relationships with Emily). The problem is, how can our relationship with God be mutual? What benefit does God derive from friendship with us? Is it not the case that in our relationship with God we are the beneficiaries of a lopsided generosity in which we can only receive and not give? If in creating us from nothing God has given us everything, what can we possibly give to God that is not already God's gift to us? Is mutuality between God and creatures possible, and if not, how is true friendship possible?

In her work *The Dialogue*, God speaks to Catherine, saying, "I ask you to love me with the same love with which I love you. But for me you cannot do this, for I loved you without being loved. Whatever love you have for me you owe me, so you love me not gratuitously but out of duty, while I love you not out of duty but gratuitously. So you cannot give me the kind of love

I ask of you." Having posed the dilemma, God then provides Catherine the answer: "This is why I have put you among your neighbors: so you can do for them what you cannot do for me—that is, love them without any concern for thanks and without looking for any profit for yourself. And whatever you do for them I will consider done for me" (chap. 64).

God identifies with our neighbor just so we can do for the neighbor what we cannot do for God, which is to love another with complete and total generosity. Moreover, it is precisely this recognition of how freely and generously we have been loved by God that inspires our free and generous love of neighbor: "Seeing that we are loved, we cannot do anything except love" (Letter 50, in O'Driscoll, *Passion for Truth*, 29).

Catherine sees a kind of triangulation of love: from God to us, from us to our neighbor, and from our neighbor back to God. In doing so, she not only shows something about our friendship with God but also shows something about our friendship with each other. While friendship, if it is true friendship, must be mutual, this cannot take the form of friends calculating how much they are giving and how much they are receiving in the friendship. True friendship must involve a kind of forgetfulness both of any benefits received and any gifts bestowed. Friendship must somehow involve both a single-minded concern to seek the good of our friend with a profound sense of gratitude for what we receive from our friend, all the while ignoring how much we give and how much we receive. Friendship is not a fifty-fifty proposition. In the mysterious mathematics of friendship, each party somehow both gives 100 percent and receives 100 percent.

In this way, human friendship dimly reflects the even more mysterious mathematics of divine-human friendship, in which God gives the creature everything, the creature gives the neighbor everything, and God rejoices always in this exchange of love. In the calculation of God, I somehow owe everything to the needy neighbor from whom I have received nothing.

*   *   *

We see a kind of negative image of the relationship between friendship with God and friendship with other people in the story of the origins of human sin in the book of Genesis. As the story begins, God and the two humans, Adam and Eve, live in harmony. The man and the woman accept each other joyfully as gifts from God. Eve is presented as the ideal partner for Adam, one drawn from his side, who is "bone of my bones and flesh of my flesh" (Gen. 2:23), truly "another self." But their grasping at equality with God, which leads to their alienation from God, also leads to their alienation from each other. When God confronts Adam with having eaten from the forbidden tree of the knowledge of good and evil, Adam responds, "The woman whom you gave to be with me, she gave me fruit from the tree, and I ate" (Gen. 3:12). In this one statement, Adam simultaneously throws Eve under the bus and manages to blame God for creating her—she who just a short time before had been "flesh of my flesh" joyfully received as gift. Eve, in turn, blames the serpent who tempted her. The scene of passing around blame is so familiar to us that it would be comical were it not for its tragic consequences. In the wake of human alienation from God, the relationship between Adam and Eve goes from being a partnership to being a matter of domination and subjection. God tells Eve, "Your desire shall be for your husband, and he shall rule over you" (Gen. 3:16). The ripple effect of this alienation extends even to humanity's relationship to the earth: Adam goes from tending the earth as a gardener to having to wrest his livelihood from the ground as if by force. "Cursed is the ground because of you; in toil you shall eat of it all the days of your life (Gen. 3:17).

The disruption of the friendship among human beings, stemming from the disruption of their friendship with God, extends down through the generations of the human family. This is perhaps most striking in the story of Cain and Abel, the first offspring of Adam and Eve. The story contains numerous themes found in the long story of human rivalry: two brothers locked in conflict; competition between sedentary farmers (Cain) and nomadic herders (Abel); people striving with each other to show themselves God's favorite. All of this is distilled in the primal homicide, in which the mutual recriminations of Adam and Eve cascade into Cain's murder of Abel. The first murder is not the killing of a stranger but of a brother. In Julian of Norwich's sense, it is the supreme act of "unkindness," a denial of human kinship. When Cain, recognizing the reverberating effect of violence, afterward expresses fear that someone might kill him in vengeance (who that could be is not exactly clear), God seeks to limit this violence by putting a mark on Cain "so that no one who came upon him would kill him" (Gen. 4:15).

The world that God blessed and declared good at the time of its creation becomes "corrupt in God's sight" and "filled with violence" (Gen. 6:11). When humans abandon God to exist in themselves, living no longer for God but for their own pleasure, they inevitably turn against one another. Catherine of Siena wrote to the civic authorities of Bologna, "Self-centered love destroys the city of the soul, and also destroys and overturns our earthly cities. . . . [N]othing has so divided the world, turning people against one another, as has self-centered love, from which injustices have sprung and still spring" (Letters 268, in O'Driscoll, *Passion for Truth*, 42). When the world is no longer seen as God's garden of abundance but as an arena of competition for limited goods—not only material goods but the goods of glory and honor and divine favor—then human beings become not gifts to each other but threats. We find ourselves in the world of "The Knight's Tale," a world of rivalry and tragic outcomes, where the face of the divine appears to us as loveless gods or indifferent fate.

The seventeenth-century philosopher and political theorist Thomas Hobbes describes the state of nature before human beings were corralled into and controlled by nation states as the "war of everyone against everyone" (*Leviathan*, chap. 13). The book of Genesis suggests something different. If we take "nature" to mean not simply the normal current state of things but the world as God created it to be, then the state of universal human warfare, no matter how common and pervasive, is profoundly *un*natural. Julian of Norwich writes, "As truly as sin is unclean, it is just as truly unkind" (*Revelations of Divine Love*, chap. 63). Sin is contrary to the kind of beings we are created to be because it deviates from God's intentions for humanity, a deviation that springs from humanity's turning from God.

If Hobbes is wrong and the book of Genesis is right, then human reconciliation with God, our return to the natural state of things, is inseparable from our reconciliation with each other. To end the war of humanity against God is to end the war of everyone against everyone.

*   *   *

God's promise to Abraham and his descendants that "in you all the families of the earth shall be blessed" (Gen. 12:3) hints that God's dealings with the Israelites will somehow bring about a restoration of the original blessing of creation, removing the curse brought about by sin. Awareness of the cosmic scope of God's promise emerges gradually, however, as the people of Israel journey through history. Not unlike the personal journey of Augustine, the collective journey of Abraham's descendants must be renarrated in light of a deepening of their historical experience of God, an experience that includes slavery in Egypt, liberation under the leadership of Moses, the conquest of the land promised to Abraham, the development of a monarchy, the collapse of that kingdom and exile in Babylon, and a partial restoration of their nation in the centuries immediately prior to the birth of Jesus.

What emerges through the course of that history is a distinctive understanding of how human beings' relationship with the divine is inextricably linked to their relationship with each other. It is not unusual for the religious beliefs of a society to mirror the social structure of that society. Sacred objects and places and times marked out by religious taboos often serve to allow members of a society to negotiate particularly fraught moments of social interaction. But the God of Israel, the God who makes a covenant with Abraham, Isaac, and Jacob, seems intensely and personally concerned with the quality of human relationships. It is not simply a case of religious taboos having a social function but of the presence of justice in human society itself taking on a religious quality so that injustice itself becomes a kind of taboo, and potential victims of injustice, particularly the widows and orphans and immigrants whom the Bible identifies as "little ones," become sacred objects.

While other ancient nations have laws that regulate the relationships of human beings with each other, ensuring that such relationships are characterized by justice and equity, Israel alone seems to understand such law (in Hebrew, Torah) as divinely given. The book of Exodus depicts the Torah being given to Moses at Mount Sinai in an awe-filled display of divine power: "there was thunder and lightning, as well as a thick cloud on the mountain, and a blast of a trumpet so loud that all the people who were in the camp trembled" (Exod. 19:16). For Israel, observance of Torah is not something alongside the worship of God; it *is* the worship of God. Torah includes what ancient people normally thought of as directives for interacting with the divine—sacrificial rituals and purity codes and sacred times and seasons—but it also includes moral injunctions concerning how the poor and widows and orphans are to be treated, what you can and cannot take as collateral for a loan, directives for dealing with slaves and immigrants, and how to punish thieves and murderers. All of this is how the people's life-giving relationship with God is to be sustained.

For many people today, religion and morality are so linked that it is difficult to imagine a world in which religion is unconcerned with morality. Even those who would say that you don't need to be religious to be moral would still think it self-evident that if you are religious you are, if not moral, at least moralistic and moralizing. Yet this is by no means presumed in the ancient world. The gods depicted in "The Knight's Tale" have a relationship with human beings that is purely transactional—they deliver benefits in exchange for worship—and seem unconcerned with the justice of relationships among humans. Mars does not care if Arcita is more just than Palamon, more deserving of Emily's hand; he simply wants Arcita to win the contest in order to show that he can deliver the goods for those who petition him. None of the gods seems concerned with the fact that Emily is being treated like a piece of property, sold to the highest bidder. The Israelites are committed, however, to the proposition that what their God desires more than sacrifice is, as the eighth-century BC prophet Micah puts it, "to do justice, and to love kindness, and to walk humbly with your God" (Mic. 6:8).

Of course, the people of Israel often fall short of this. They are constantly tempted to treat their God as if he were like the transactional gods of other peoples, desirous of sacrifice but indifferent to justice. Micah denounces the Israelites who "abhor justice and pervert all equity" (Mic. 3:9) and yet think that God can be bought off with a few slaughtered sheep and bulls. The religious and political leaders of Jerusalem, Israel's royal city, come in for particularly harsh criticism for both their corruption and their arrogant presumption of God's favor:

> Its rulers give judgement for a bribe,
>> its priests teach for a price,
>> its prophets give oracles for money;
> yet they lean upon the LORD and say,
>>> "Surely the LORD is with us!
>>> No harm shall come upon us." (Mic. 3:11)

The sharp denunciations of prophets like Micah are intended to cut the people to the heart and bring them back into friendship with God. But the measure of this friendship with God is always the existence of just and loving relationships among human beings. The care of the little ones who are defenseless is the criterion of justice.

Micah and the other prophets believe that this way of living is the natural state of human existence, not the war of everyone against everyone. And if God's covenant people live with each other and with God in this way, if they live according to God's loving-kindness, God will bless them with life, and the other families of the earth will see this blessing and come to the holy city of Jerusalem to learn how to live in this same way. Living at peace with God and each other is what people most deeply desire; it is inherently attractive because it is the kind of life for which we were created. Learning to live in this way means an end to fallenness and fratricide, violence and vengeance. Micah prophesies that God

> shall judge between many peoples,
>> and shall arbitrate between strong nations
>>> far away;

> they shall beat their swords into ploughshares,
> and their spears into pruning-hooks;
> nation shall not lift up sword against nation,
> neither shall they learn war any more.
> (Mic. 4:3)

God declares a truce in the war of everyone against everyone by pouring out the Spirit of wisdom and making the human race into prophets and friends of God, and therefore friends of each other. It is a glorious vision. It is a vision that awaits fulfillment.

*   *   *

Earlier I wrote that the claim that Jesus is the Messiah of Israel identifies him as the one who will fulfill the promise made to Abraham that in him all the families of the earth would find blessing. We might say that the glorious vision of the truce of God, the end of the war of everyone against everyone, which Micah and the other prophets proclaim, comes to pass in Jesus. When Jesus commands his followers to love, he is not replacing Torah but going to its heart. This is why he says, "Do not think that I have come to abolish the law or the prophets; I have come not to abolish but to fulfill" (Matt. 5:17). At the same time, in fulfilling Torah Jesus radicalizes its demands, as if to force the issue of just where the limits of love are.

Matthew's Gospel conveys this radicalizing of Torah by depicting Jesus preaching to the crowd from the top of a mountain, mirroring Moses's journey up Mt. Sinai to receive the law from God. Jesus tells them that their righteousness must exceed that of the teachers of Torah and then launches into a series of statements of the form, "You have heard it said . . . but *I* say to you." Thus, Torah says not to murder, but Jesus says we should not even be angry or utter harsh words; Torah says not to commit adultery, but Jesus says we must free our lives from even lustful thoughts; Torah says that in taking vengeance we should not exceed the damage done to us, but Jesus says not to retaliate at all. In each case, Jesus takes what is said in Torah and presses home a call to an even higher standard of justice and mercy, an even wider scope to love.

This pattern culminates in Jesus saying to the crowd, "You have heard that it was said, 'You shall love your neighbor and hate your enemy.' But I say to you, love your enemies and pray for those who persecute you" (Matt. 5:43–44). As Matthew presents it, Jesus's command to love extends not just to those whom we are inclined to love or even simply to those toward whom we are neutral, but even to those who hate us and wish us harm. The reason we must love not just friends but also enemies is that in doing so we imitate God, who "makes his sun rise on the evil and on the good, and sends rain on the righteous and the unrighteous" (Matt. 5:45). If, as Aristotle said, true friends desire the same good, and if God desires good for even the unrighteous, then we too must desire the good of our enemies if we are to be friends of God.

This love of enemies is connected to the persistent teaching of the New Testament that we must forgive others if we ourselves wish to be forgiven. The prayer that Jesus teaches to his disciples asks, "Forgive us our debts, as we also have forgiven our debtors" (Matt. 6:12), which Jesus immediately expands upon: "For if you forgive others their trespasses, your heavenly Father will also forgive you; but if you do not forgive others, neither will your Father forgive your trespasses" (Matt. 6:14). In Luke's Gospel Jesus says, "Do not judge, and you will not be judged; do not condemn, and you will not be condemned. Forgive, and you will be forgiven" (Luke 6:37). Paul reverses the link between forgiving and being forgiven. Rather than our forgiveness of others being a precondition for God's forgiveness of us, Paul sees our forgiveness of others flowing from our imitation of the example given by God in forgiving us: "Bear with one another and, if anyone has a complaint against another, forgive each other; just as the Lord has forgiven you, so you also must forgive" (Col. 3.13); "be kind to one another, tender-hearted, forgiving one another, as God in Christ has forgiven you" (Eph. 4:32).

But whether we start with God's forgiveness of us or our forgiveness of others, the point is that the two are so linked that we cannot possess one without the other. If God has forgiven us, we *must* forgive others; otherwise we become unlike God, and our friendship with God cannot be sustained. As the Rev. Martin Luther King Jr. said in the midst of the civil rights struggle of the 1960s, "We must love our enemies, because only by loving them can we know God and experience the beauty of his holiness" (*Strength to Love*, 50).

*　　*　　*

Christian teaching on forgiveness and love of enemies is in some ways both the most attractive aspect of Christianity and the most repellant. We like the idea of being forgiven, whether by God or by those whom we have hurt. We might even like, in theory, the idea that we can be like God by forgiving others without reserve. We like it, that is, until we begin to think of who our enemies are and what they have done. We like it as long as we can keep the enemy an abstract, unspecified enemy. But the memory of specific harms inflicted on us and on those whom we love can block the flow of forgiveness. And, in some ways, it should. For while we may be free to forgive the harm our enemies have inflicted on us, are we equally free to forgive the harm inflicted on those whom we love? Is it not a violation of divine justice to let evil people off the hook for the evil they have done, whether to us or to others? What sort of God would demand such a thing?

A belief in the impossibility or wrongness of forgiving enemies who have harmed those whom we love may be the best possible reason to reject the Christian faith. To reject such forgiveness as possible at all is to reject the faith that love can be without boundaries, which is to reject faith in a God whose very nature is love. To reject such forgiveness as a possibility for human beings is to reject the faith that unbounded love has become human flesh and dwelt among us in Jesus Christ, becoming the crucified love that even on the cross prays, "Father, forgive them; for they do not know what they are doing" (Luke 23:34). To reject such forgiveness as morally wrong is to reject the faith that the Holy Spirit calls us to be friends of the risen Jesus, loving what he loves, forgiving what he forgives. Jesus's teaching on love of enemies and forgiveness of wrongdoers may lead us to say, as some erstwhile followers of Jesus said in a different context, "This teaching is difficult; who can accept it?" (John 6:60). If that is the case, then at least we are rejecting the authentic heart of the Christian faith and not some distorted cultural image of it that presents Christians as believing in a self-interested god or seeing the cross as a source of guilt or seeing our relationship to God as a transactional one.

Of course, loving our enemies and forgiving them is not the same thing as overlooking injustice. Jesus warns against judging others; he does not forbid making moral judgments. Indeed, the imperative to love our enemies suggests a correlative imperative to recognize them *as* enemies, to pass unsentimental judgment on how and why their actions are wrong and harmful so we know the appropriate way to show them love. Augustine meditates on the verse from Psalm 139 that says, "I have hated them with perfect hatred" (v. 22), wondering how this could fit with Jesus's command to love even our enemies. He writes that just as one has a duty to love one's enemies, there is also a duty to hate and denounce what is evil in them, while loving in them the foundation of divinely created goodness on which their evil feeds like a parasite: "he should not hate the person because of the fault, nor should he love the fault because of the person. He should hate the fault but love the man" (*City of God* 14.7). To hate our enemies with perfect hatred is to love them in the deepest way possible; it is to reject their evil and seek to heal it without surrendering our love for them as God's creation; it is to hope that our enemies are destroyed by becoming our friends through the transforming work of God's mercy, a mercy shown to us and to them alike.

*   *   *

I have a friend who visibly winces whenever the subject of lov-ing enemies comes up. She is someone who is committed to a life of prophetic advocacy for the poor and vulnerable, and who hates hypocrisy and selfishness and willful ignorance of the plight of others. She winces because she knows that the love of enemies truly lies at the heart of Christianity. She winces because she knows that the only love that can encom-pass even our enemy is the love that has been stretched out and broken open on the cross: love that makes itself vulnerable to the hatred of enemies believing that love is stronger than hate and that life will triumph over death. She winces because she knows that friendship with Jesus means sharing in this crucified love.

I said earlier that Jesus's followers were not very keen on the notion of a messiah who had to be crucified. As if to add insult to injury, after predicting his death, Jesus goes on to say to them, "If any want to become my followers, let them deny themselves and take up their cross and follow me" (Mark 8:34). Jesus's words are echoed in the first letter of John: "We know love by this, that he laid down his life for us—and we ought to lay down our lives for one another" (1 John 3:16). Friendship with the crucified Messiah involves sharing in his fate, laying down your life in dramatic and not-so-dramatic ways. Ignacio Ellacuría notes that the Christian's "mystical" dying and ris-ing with Jesus in baptism "bring consequences like those Jesus suffered, as long as the world remains like the world in which Jesus lived" (*Essays on History, Liberation, and Salvation*, 233).

The early-second-century bishop Ignatius of Antioch, as he journeyed under guard toward execution in Rome, wrote to those seeking to persuade him to find a way to avoid death, "To die in Jesus Christ is better than to be monarch of earth's widest bounds. He who dies for us is all I seek; He who rose again is my whole desire. . . . Leave me to imitate the Passion of my God" (*Letter to the Romans* 6). To willingly take up the cross is to follow Jesus's path of striving only for the kingdom of God; it is to throw your life into the abyss of love, trusting in God's power to bear you up.

This becomes particularly clear in loving our enemies. Embracing the cross is both the precondition that makes possible love of our enemies and the inevitable consequence of such love. If the cross of Jesus teaches us anything, it is that love of enemies will often be perceived as weakness by those enemies, a weakness that they will not hesitate to exploit. The enemies we love may well be the ones who make sure that our lives take the form of crucified love. To take up the cross is to renounce self-protection.

Taking up the cross in love of both friend and enemy involves a still-more-wrenching renunciation: the renunciation of the illusion that we can protect our friends from our enemies. To hate our enemies with perfect hatred is to accept limits on the means we can use to protect ourselves and those we love. As deep as our commitment to justice may be, we cannot pursue justice by utterly destroying the unjust. Or, rather, our only means of destroying the unjust is to make them just, enticing them into friendship with God by letting our witness of love be the instrument of God's grace. Martin Luther King

Jr. said to those who opposed desegregation, "Be ye assured that we will wear you down with our capacity to suffer. One day we shall win freedom, but not only for ourselves. We shall so appeal to your heart and conscience that we shall win *you* in the process, and our victory will be a double victory" (*Strength to Love*, 51). To love our enemies is to renounce the idea that we have it in our power to make history turn out right, to end all suffering, to banish all evil. To love our enemies is, in the end, to disarm ourselves of any weapons except the cross and the Spirit's gifts of faith, hope, and love.

To speak of renouncing the aspiration to make history turn out right might sound like a counsel to sit on our hands as we wait for God to fix things. But this is not, in fact, the lesson that followers of Jesus have drawn. The first letter of John says, "Little children, let us love, not in word or speech, but in truth and action" (1 John 3:18). To love is to take action. To love our neighbors who are suffering is both to work to alleviate their suffering and also to denounce the cause of their suffering, to make their enemies our enemies and as such the object of our love. But those who seek most resolutely to put love into action are also those who recognize most clearly their own incapacity to control outcomes.

In Fyodor Dostoyevsky's novel *The Brothers Karamazov*, the holy man Father Zosima, speaking to a well-intentioned and well-to-do woman who finds it easy to love people in theory but difficult in practice, says, "Active love is a harsh and fearful thing compared with love in dreams. Love in dreams thirsts for immediate action, quickly performed, and with everyone watching. Indeed, it will go as far as giving even of one's life, provided it does not take long but is soon over, as on stage, and everyone is looking on and praising. Whereas active love is labor and perseverance, and for some people, perhaps, a whole science" (bk. 2, chap. 4).

Love is a work of patience, and to practice patience is to suffer the flow of time, recognizing our incapacity to rush redemption. The trick is to work ceaselessly, putting love into action in the most concrete ways possible, while simultaneously leaving the outcome of our labor entirely in the hands of God.

*   *   *

The kind of abstract love for humanity in general that Father Zosima denounces as "love in dreams" is a persistent temptation for those who seek to follow Jesus's command to love. Because this is a command of universal scope—a love of both friends and enemies, of neighbors both near and far—it can easily fall prey to a vagueness that dulls the sharp edge of the harsh and fearful love that Jesus calls us to. But how can we have such love for billions of people, almost none of whom we shall ever meet? Aristotle said that it was characteristic of friends to live together, and while it is undeniably true that we all inhabit an increasingly fragile and interconnected earth, it is pretty clear that Aristotle thought friendship involved something more robust than a shared global concern and social media "friendships."

Perhaps it only within a smaller circle of friendship that we can learn a love that might one day blossom forth into that love of both friend and enemy, of near and far neighbor, the end to the war of everyone against everyone that Jesus commands. While Jesus taught a love that is universal, he also showed particular concern for the "little flock" of his followers (Luke 12:32), for it is within this community that we are formed as lovers of God and neighbor. This little flock is what we call "church."

Further Reading

- The book of Micah. This eight-century BC Hebrew prophet sounds many of the same themes as the much-longer book of the prophet Isaiah: denunciation of social injustice and idolatry; warning of God's impending judgment on the Israelites; and a promise of future vindication and restoration by God.

- Mary O'Driscoll (ed.), *Catherine of Siena: Passion for the Truth, Compassion for Humanity*. This collection of writings by the fourteenth-century mystic and prophet Catherine is drawn from her letters, prayers, and other writings. It presents a brief but representative sampling of her thought, showing the link she forges between love of God and active love of neighbor.

5

*We live our love out from the community
created by the Spirit.*

It is hardly news that in the past hundred years, the developed world has seen massive and ongoing defections from Christianity. This began in Europe, where Christianity is at the heart of the origins of European culture and institutions but is increasingly abandoned. About 51 percent of the citizens of France identify as Christian, down from about 80 percent thirty years ago, with only about 25 percent of those under thirty identifying as Christian. When one looks at religious practice, the state of institutional Christianity seems even more dire: among those French who identify as Catholics, for example, Sunday Mass attendance is below 5 percent. The United States, long thought to be more religious than Europe, has recently seen the beginnings of a similar decline. While 78 percent of those between fifty and sixty-five identify as Christian, only 55 percent of those from eighteen to twenty-nine do so, and 36 percent identify as having no religious affiliation. Among the young unaffiliated, only about a third identify as atheist or agnostic; the rest are simply "nothing in particular." These are the "nones," like my friend who saw in the crucifixion only a debilitating source of guilt. Some of these young people might acquire a religious affiliation as they get older, particularly when they begin to form their own families, but it is hard to avoid the impression that more and more people are happy to have a fairly vague religious identity, to be "spiritual but not religious," as they say.

Christians might take solace in the rapid and continued growth of churches in Africa and parts of Asia, but this does not change the fact of a collapse of identification with religious institutions in Europe and North America. I am not qualified to offer anything more than untutored speculation as to what accounts for this, so I will spare you that. What is a more pressing question for me is why those who affirm what has been said up to this point—that God is love, that the love that is God is crucified love, that we are called to be friends with the risen Jesus, and that we cannot love God without loving each other—might think that the Holy Spirit calls them to commit themselves to a concrete community of people who share that faith.

*   *   *

The English word *church* is how we translate the Greek word *ekklēsia*, which could also be translated as "assembly" or "gathering," suggesting a group of people who have been called together for a particular purpose. The calling together of the church is rooted first in God's calling of Abraham and his descendants to be "a priestly kingdom and a holy nation" (Exod. 19:6), as well as in Jesus's calling of his disciples, especially an inner circle of twelve, "whom he also named apostles, to be with him, and to be sent out to proclaim the message" (Mark 3:14). But the New Testament typically uses the term *church* for those people who have been called together by the Spirit after the resurrection of Jesus. And the Spirit seems to have made some rather surprising choices.

A central theme of both the book of the Acts of the Apostles and of Paul's letters is how the Spirit, apparently against all expectations, decided that the community of God's people, the friends with whom God has made a covenant in the blood of the crucified Messiah, will be a community of both Jews and Gentiles (i.e., anyone who is not Jewish). That is, it will no longer be restricted to those who are descended from Abraham and follow the Torah given to Moses but will now encompass anyone who has faith in Jesus crucified and risen. This might seem an arcane issue buried in the irrelevance of history, but I believe it speaks to the deep divisions that afflict our world to this day, the ongoing war of everyone against everyone, the conflicts between nations, political parties, races, and social and economic classes. We see these divisions in the small number of noisy advocates for ethno-nationalism, and the far larger number of citizens who fear that foreign immigrants will spread crime or destroy our economy. We see them in the way that systems of justice are contoured along lines of race and class to advantage some groups and disadvantage others, in many cases fatally. The first-century struggle for a church of Jews and Gentiles speaks to the struggles of our own world for peace and justice and to the church's place in that struggle.

In the Acts of the Apostles, the Spirit, having initially been poured out on the apostles on the day of Pentecost, empowering them to speak in unknown languages (Acts 2:4), begins to manifest its presence among Gentiles. In a significant turn of events, an angel appears to the Gentile centurion Cornelius and commands him to send for Peter. Peter, instructed by the Spirt, goes to Cornelius and his household. When Peter preaches to them, proclaiming the fulfillment of the promises to Israel through the death and resurrection of Jesus, "the Holy Spirit fell upon all who heard the word" (Acts 10:44), and Cornelius and his household receive the same capacity to speak unknown languages that the disciples did on Pentecost. This serves as a sign to Peter that they too can be baptized and numbered among the friends of God, even if they have not been keeping all the rules of Torah: "Can anyone withhold the water for baptizing these people who have received the Holy Spirit just as we have?" (Acts 10:47). The radical nature of the Spirit's act of Gentile inclusion, and Peter's acceptance of it, is disturbing to many of the first Christians, who have presumed that Jesus is a Jewish Messiah, sent for Jewish salvation, and that those outside of the law of Moses were somehow "unclean." It is only after a contentious meeting in Jerusalem, held in response both to Peter's bold act and to Paul's growing ministry among Gentiles in Antioch, that the leaders of the early Christian movement determine that the Holy Spirit truly is at work and that Gentiles can become part of their community without being required to keep the whole of Torah.

We can easily forget the sharp distinction between Jews and Gentiles that existed in the first century, a distinction that was reinforced from both sides of the divide. Paul's letter to the Ephesians gives some sense of how Gentiles were viewed by Jews, telling the Gentiles of the church of Ephesus that prior to receiving Christ they were "aliens from the commonwealth of Israel, and strangers to the covenants of promise, having no hope and without God in the world" (Eph. 2:12). From the first-century Jewish perspective, Gentiles were not unlike pigs or other unclean animals: having a Gentile *at* the table is as defiling as having pork *on* the table. Though Abraham is called into friendship with God in order to fulfill God's purpose of blessing *all* of the families of the earth, the division between Jew and non-Jew seems over time to have become one more battle line in the war of everyone against everyone. Jesus, however, declares peace between them: "in his flesh he has made both groups into one and has broken down the dividing wall, that is, the hostility between us" (v. 14). The Gentiles, through faith in Jesus and the calling of the Spirit, "are no longer strangers and aliens, but . . . citizens with the saints and also members of the household of God" (v. 19). This being the case, Paul exhorts them "to lead a life worthy of the calling to which you have been called, with all humility and gentleness, with patience, bearing with one another in love, making every effort to maintain the unity of the Spirit in the bond of peace" (Eph. 4:1-3).

One of the dominant images used by Paul in speaking of this bond of peace established by the Spirit is that of the body of Christ. This is a rich notion that Paul deploys in a variety of ways. In writing to the Christians of Corinth as well as those of Rome, he uses the unity of the diverse parts of the human body to speak of how the diverse gifts given by the Spirit within the church should not divide the church but unite it in its diversity: "For just as the body is one and has many members, and all the members of the body, though many, are one body, so it is with Christ. For in the one Spirit we were all baptized into one body" (1 Cor. 12:12-13). In writing to Christians in Colossae, Paul uses the image of the body to underscore the unity between the church and Jesus, who is the head of the body, "from whom the whole body, nourished and held together by its ligaments and sinews, grows with a growth that is from God" (Col. 2:19). For the Christians of Ephesus Paul draws together imagery of diversity of members, union with Christ the head, and growth in love: "speaking the truth in love, we must grow up in every way into him who is the head, into Christ, from whom the whole body, joined and knitted together by every ligament with which it is equipped, as each part is working properly, promotes the body's growth in building itself up in love" (Eph. 4:15-16).

The household of God, dwelling as one without the dividing wall between Jew and Gentile, slave and free, male and female, rich and poor, wise and simple, is to live as a sign of the kingdom Jesus proclaimed, a pocket of resistance to the universal warfare that was born in the devastation of Eden's garden, a down payment on God's promise proclaimed through the prophets that swords would be beaten into ploughshares and spears into pruning hooks, the site within human history where enemies are transformed into friends through the Spirit.

*   *   *

All of this might give the impression that the early community called together by the Spirit was some sort of idyllic utopia: that the Gentile lion dwelled peacefully with the Jewish lamb, that the human tendency toward self-love was banished, that the war of everyone against everyone was suddenly at an end. This impression would be mistaken. The New Testament is remarkably frank in its depiction of the internal struggles of the early Christian *ekklēsia*. I have already mentioned the resistance Peter and Paul encounter in response to the Spirit's radical work of including Gentiles within God's covenant. Old patterns of thinking die hard, and the idea that the identity of God's friends is no longer tied to being a descendant of Abraham but to possessing the kind of faith possessed by Abraham proves to be a difficult one to acquire.

Paul unleashes his harshest invective in writing to the Christians of Galatia, who have let interlopers come into their community who tell them that friendship with God requires full observance of Torah, particularly circumcision of all males. For Paul, this puts a human action, rather than God's action through Jesus and the Spirit, at the heart of our friendship with God. He sees those who preach the necessity of circumcision as enemies of Jesus's saving work on the cross, even if they claim the name Christian, and suggests that those who are so keen on circumcision should go all-in: "I wish those who unsettle you would castrate themselves!" (Gal. 5:12). Paul is so strident in his opposition not because he thinks there is something inherently wrong with circumcision. The problem with insistence on circumcision is that it is a sign of being locked into the old pattern of thinking that had divided the world into Jew and Gentile, and of being blind to the new thing that the Spirit is doing: "neither circumcision nor uncircumcision is anything; but a new creation is everything!" (Gal. 6:15).

But it is not only Jewish Christians who are locked into old patterns. Gentile Christians, lacking the centuries-long formation of life lived under Torah, could easily treat the God revealed in Jesus as one of those transactional gods of pagan antiquity, who provide benefits in exchange for worship, but who make no deep moral demands on us. Paul tells the Gentiles in Galatia, who seem to have resumed certain pagan ritual observances, "when you did not know God, you were enslaved to beings that by nature are not gods. . . . How can you want to be enslaved to them again? . . . I am afraid that my work for you may have been wasted" (Gal. 4:8-9, 11). The church is not free from the allure of a god who is not love but an impersonal dispenser of benefits to those who pay the proper price.

Alongside the persistence of former patterns of thinking, there is also the usual supply of garden variety human selfishness. The first letter of John reminds its readers, "If we say that we have no sin, we deceive ourselves, and the truth is not in us" (1 John 1:8). The letter of James is even more pointed in describing the sins of Christians: "Those conflicts and disputes among you, where do they come from? Do they not come from your cravings that are at war within you? You want something and do not have it; so you commit murder. And you covet something and cannot obtain it; so you engage in disputes and conflicts" (James 4:1-2).

Paul's correspondence with the Christians of Corinth displays a similar tale of unsavory behavior, including greed, legal disputes, class conflict, and at least one case of incest. Whatever else one might want to say about the Bible's depiction of the early Christian community, one cannot say that it is an idealized one. The unity of Christ's body seems to have been a work in progress and something less than complete unanimity.

*　　*　　*

What does all this ancient history about Jews and Gentiles have to say to those who are spiritual but not religious, who have disaffiliated from the visible structures of the Christian faith and think, not without reason, that their Sunday mornings may be better spent hiking in the woods or having a leisurely brunch rather than enduring badly sung hymns and a poorly thought-out sermon that rehashes moralistic business as usual, often simply retracing the dividing lines of secular party politics? Among other things, the Spirit's formation of the church of Jews and Gentiles suggests that part of being a friend of God involves being part of a visible community in which reconciliation of enemies takes bodily form through specific practices. It suggests a need for a space of face-to-face confrontation with those who, apart from God's friendship, would be strangers and aliens to us. It suggests that we need to be not simply "spiritual" but also "religious."

Our word *religion* comes from the Latin *religare*, meaning "to bind together." In rejecting religion in favor of spirituality, even those who do not know or care about the etymology of words sense that religion is a binding thing, a kind of constriction placed on the freedom of the individual spirit. The ancient Romans referred to their public rituals, in which sacrifice was offered to the gods of the city, as "religion" because these were acts that bound the citizens of Rome together as a people. The Romans did not particularly care if you *believed* in the gods of the city, much less *loved* them, but only that you participated in the rituals that implored their favor. Indeed, one of the reasons why the Romans were so puzzled by the early Christian refusal to participate in these sacrifices, and persecuted them for that refusal, was that they saw them simply as civic rituals that formed people into one community—not unlike pledging allegiance to the flag or cooking hotdogs on Independence Day. They were ways of partially containing the war of everyone against everyone by drawing a subset of humanity into a common identity.

When early Christians rejected the religion of Rome (which is one reason they were accused of being atheists), they did not do so in the name of spirituality. Rather, they rejected the religion—the binding—that Rome sought to impose on them in the name of the bonds that the Spirit imposed on them. If the story of the calling of Cornelius and other Gentiles into friendship with God in the body of Christ tells us anything, it is that you don't get to choose who it is that the Spirit puts you with. Much of the friction we find in the early years of the church arises precisely from the fact that the *ekklēsia* is not an affinity group, a voluntary association of individuals, but rather a point of convergence to which people have been impelled by the driving wind of the Holy Spirit. Jesus says to Nicodemus, "The wind [Spirit/*pneuma*] blows where it chooses, and you hear the sound of it, but you do not know where it comes from or where it goes. So it is with everyone who is born of the Spirit" (John 3:8). The church, rather than being an association of like-minded people, is more likely to be a group of people you would never choose to be friends with if they were not also friends of Jesus. Paul sees his fellow Christians as something less than the cream of the crop: "not many of you were wise by human standards, not many were powerful, not many were of noble birth" (1 Cor. 1:26). In Aristotle's terms, they are often neither useful nor pleasant. When the Spirit binds us together in the church, it is often with people whom we find unappealing, unhelpful, unlovely—the kind of person we might see at a party and think, "Who invited *him*?"

Over time, the church did become the domain of clever, powerful, and wealthy people. But this seems only to have made the church more fraught with divisions, as such people often sought to use the church for their own purposes, to prop up existing power structures. One need not think long to come up with examples of the church's exceedingly comfortable relationship with power down through the centuries. Suppression of dissent, wars fought in the name of Christ, forced conversions, abuse of clerical power and privilege—all of these things are realities of the church's story. But are they the whole story?

Dorothy Day, the radical journalist who converted to Catholicism in 1927 and became one of modern Christianity's most resolute advocates for the poor and disenfranchised, passionately loved the church but often found herself at odds with Christians who were comfortable with the status quo. She wrote, "I loved the Church for Christ made visible. Not for itself, because it was so often a scandal to me. Romano Guardini said the Church is the Cross on which Christ was crucified; one could not separate Christ from his cross, and one must live in a state of perpetual dissatisfaction with the Church" (*Long Loneliness*, 149–50).

Day's pacifism put her at odds with bishops who blessed battleships, and her labor radicalism put her at odds with a priesthood that had made peace with plutocracy. Yet despite her lifelong dissatisfaction with the church, Day found the rituals and community and even the institutions of Catholicism sustaining and life-giving. A few years before her death in 1980, she made this clear in an address she delivered to a gathering in Philadelphia: "It was also the physical aspect of the Church which attracted me. Bread and wine, water (all water is made holy since Christ was baptized in the Jordan), incense, the sound of waves and wind, all nature cried out to me. My love and gratitude to the Church have grown through the years. She was my mother and nourished me, and taught me. She taught me the crowning love of the life of the Spirit" ("Bread for the Hungry," 2).

It was precisely those most "religious" aspects of Catholicism that made Christ visible for Day and bound her to the fellow Christians whom she often found so trying. It is precisely in repetitive rituals that the slow work of binding human beings together takes place: rituals of washing, eating, drinking, anointing, touching, singing, truth-telling. It is in these repeated actions, engaged in together by human beings, that the worship of God takes place. She compares them to the exchange of a morning and evening kiss between spouses, which might seem to be a meaningless ritual but which "on occasion turns to rapture, a burning fire of tenderness and love" (*Long Loneliness*, 200). For Day, the routine of shared religious practice provides the seedbed from which the Spirit might blossom forth.

So perhaps the answer to the widespread disillusion that many, particularly young people, feel toward the church is not less religion and more spirituality but in fact more religion, more habit, more ritual. That is to say, in a divided and lonely world those who have been called into friendship with Jesus need to be, even in their differences, *more* bound to each other, not less. The world needs a people who are so closely bound together by the God who is love that they can afford to differ from and with each other and yet still meet at the table of the Eucharist, the feast of their friendship in Christ. The seer John of Patmos records in the book of Revelation a vision of the friends of God, gathered into God's kingdom at the end of time: "I looked, and there was a great multitude that no one could count, from every nation, from all tribes and peoples and languages, standing before the throne and before the Lamb, robed in white, with palm branches in their hands. They cried out in a loud voice, saying, 'Salvation belongs to our God who is seated on the throne, and to the Lamb!'" (Rev. 7:9-10).

This vision echoes that of the prophets, who saw all the nations of the world coming to worship the one true God and learn the ways of peace. The Eucharist of the church, celebrated amid the divisions of the world, is an embodied foretaste of the kingdom, a banquet that makes possible a friendship that dissolves the boundaries of nation and tribe and language, of race and class and gender, rebinding humanity into the one body of Christ, composed of a multitude of members joined together in worship of God.

*   *   *

If the Eucharist is the visible practice by which Christians celebrate their ongoing friendship with each other in Christ, baptism is the practice that establishes their fundamental identity, the ritual act that first binds them to that community of divine friendship. Writing to the Christians of Galatia, Paul points to the ritual of baptism as both binding and boundary-breaching: "As many of you as were baptized into Christ have clothed yourselves with Christ. There is no longer Jew or Greek, there is no longer slave or free, there is no longer male and female; for all of you are one in Christ Jesus" (Gal. 3:27-28). Paul suggests that people entering the waters of baptism leave behind an old identity and acquire a new one. Boundaries of ethnicity, social status, and even gender are washed away in a bath that is both a death and a birth. Stripped of all former status, one emerges now clothed in Christ, enveloped in a new identity. Most baptisms in the early Christian centuries involved being stripped naked, fully immersed in water, and then reclothed, so the imagery Paul uses would have been particularly resonant for early Christians, more than for those who associate baptism with a few drops of water being poured over a baby's head. The baptismal ritual of the early church was nothing if not dramatic.

It was also terribly undignified. Even today, baptisms are often undignified affairs, despite our best efforts to tame the blowing of the Spirit. Whether it is a matter of spluttering adults emerging from a muddy river or squalling babies squirming at a stone font, baptisms tend to be messy. But should we expect it to be otherwise? If it is the case, as Paul says, that we are saved by "the water of rebirth and renewal by the Holy Spirit" (Titus 3:5) and that "all of us who have been baptized into Christ Jesus were baptized into his death" (Rom. 6:3), then it is only fitting that the ritual of baptism should convey the messy reality of both birth and death. Neither gaining nor losing an identity is ever neatly accomplished. Yet the indignity of baptism is for the sake of gaining a new, deeper, and truer dignity: the dignity of those who have become friends of the God who is love. Notions of dignity based on the superiority of a particular race or class or gender are a barrier to experiencing joy; they are so fragile in their falsity that we must expend great energy anxiously preserving them and propping them up. Only when they collapse and we find a new identity in the crucified love of Jesus, dying and rising with him in the waters of new birth, can a dignity that engenders joy be found. At the same time, this new identity in Christ does not obliterate the differences between Christians; variations of cultural and racial and sexual identity rise reborn from the waters of baptism, no longer a source of division but enriching the diversity of the body of Christ.

Needless to say, the church often fails to live up to what the ritual of baptism promises. Though Paul says that in Christ there is no longer slave or free, it took many long centuries before slaveholding Christians came to understand that friendship in the body of Christ was incompatible with the practice of slaveholding (something that had long been apparent to the slaves who embraced Christianity). Though Paul says that in Christ there is neither male nor female, and despite the important role women have played throughout the history of the church, women are often still relegated to subordinate roles in many Christian communities and homes, often bolstered by appeal to the teachings of Paul himself. The common bonds of baptism have not kept Christians from slaughtering each other in war, sometimes even in the name of the God who is love, or from exploiting each other economically, or from seeing racial identity as more important than unity in Christ. Perhaps most of all, the church is too often anxious and joyless, as if the gates of hell could, contrary to Jesus's promise, prevail against it (Matt. 16:18), and from this anxiety and sorrow flows the grasping at security and power that so plagues the church. The church should, of course, follow Jesus's counsel to "be wise as serpents and innocent as doves" (Matt. 10:16) in navigating a hostile world, but too often the balance of wisdom and innocence in the church has inclined more to the serpent than to the dove, and the church strives more for the things of this world than for the kingdom. Yet it is this same church that carries within it the profoundly subversive ritual of death by water, a ritual from which, despite our attempts to domesticate it, can burst forth the hurricane force of the Spirit's joy.

*   *   *

Some people associate the word *tradition*, like the word *religion*, with stultifying constriction and unquestioning support of the status quo. But the example of the radical potential of baptism to reconfigure identities and breach boundaries suggests that the traditions carried within the life of the church can also subvert the status quo and liberate people from the tyranny of the present. Even—perhaps especially—those traditions that seem initially most unintelligible to our current way of thinking can challenge us to think in new ways, giving the witness of Christians a critical edge against those things that are presumed to go without saying in our culture. In an odd sort of paradox that seems entirely fitting when we are dealing with a God who transcends time, the voices of the past can be precisely those voices that call us into future. When Christians profess belief in the "communion of saints," they are saying that God's friends of the past are living still; like the risen Jesus himself, they are more alive than we are, because they possess a clearer vision of the kingdom toward which we still journey.

All human traditions serve to locate us in the world, and this may be a good thing or a bad thing, depending on that location. Traditions that locate us in places of untruth, indignity, and conflict are traditions of death. But the authentic tradition of the gospel, the true handing-on of Jesus's proclamation of the kingdom, as this has been lived down through the centuries by great saints and ordinary Christians, is a tradition of life, because it locates us in a place of truth and justice, dignity and kindness. It is not always easy to discern that authentic tradition, though the story of Israel, Jesus, and the apostles as recounted in Scripture certainly can serve as a starting point in our discernment. The lives of the saints, those exemplary friends of God, so varied in time and circumstance yet partaking of the one Spirit, can help us see the diversity of ways in which people have sought to hand on the good news. So too can conversation with our fellow Christians today, in particular those with whom we disagree, whom we are inclined to see as strangers and aliens. Indeed, tradition is not so much a body of propositions to be believed or fixed practices to be carried out as it is a vast and sprawling conversation extended across time and space in which we discern together where the Spirit is blowing.

When we speak of tradition, we inevitably also speak of institutions, since traditions are borne by institutions. And in speaking of institutions, we must speak also of authority. A friend of mine, in answer to complaints about the institutional church or organized religion, used to say, "Everyone who has a house lives on a street, and every street is in a neighborhood, and every neighborhood is in a town, and every town has a mayor." In others words, institutions are inevitable whenever you have a group of people trying to accomplish some common end. One reason the institutional aspect of Christianity, whether in the form of the Vatican or the Southern Baptist Convention or a local pastor, is often the least attractive face of the church is that concern for institutional maintenance, as necessary as it may be, can often override answering the call of the Spirit. But institutions and authority can also serve such salutary spiritual ends as feeding the hungry, caring for the sick, sheltering the stranger, or instructing the ignorant. Because the church is a movement of peoples within human history aimed at a common goal, it is not a question of *whether* the church should take institutional form or *whether* authority should be exercised, but *how*.

John Henry Newman wrote of the process of discerning the truth within the Catholic Church in terms of a fruitful tension between "authority" and "private judgment"—two great forces "alternately advancing and retreating as the ebb and flow of the tide." The church "is a vast assemblage of human beings with willful intellects and wild passions, brought together into one" under a common authority in a kind of school of discernment, "not as if into a hospital or into a prison, not in order to be sent to bed, not to be buried alive, but (if I may change my metaphor) brought together as if into some moral factory, for the melting, refining, and moulding, by an incessant, noisy process, of the raw material of human nature, so excellent, so dangerous, so capable of divine purposes" (*Apologia pro Vita Sua*, chap. 5).

Newman pillages the imagery of nineteenth-century industrialization in order to make his point, and perhaps we might prefer to reimagine that "moral factory" as a worker-owned and eco-friendly enterprise, but the grimy metaphor of the Victorian factory captures some of the messiness, but also the majesty, of tradition—its bedlam but also its beauty. For him, the tradition of the church locates us in the heart of that messy majesty, that beautiful bedlam that is the wildness of the Spirit.

*   *   *

Still, we perhaps have not yet gotten to the heart of the issue for at least some of those who choose to remain spiritual but not religious. Questions remain. Isn't all this talk about friendship in Christ and a new identity and belonging to a tradition simply, in the end, exclusionary? Do Christians not claim to have a monopoly on friendship with God? If God is love, then does God not love all people regardless of their religion or lack of religion? Put most baldly, do you have to be a Christian in order to be saved?

Perhaps the first thing to say, though it really should go without saying, is that the determination of anyone's salvation is God's concern and not ours, and the visible boundaries of the church in history are not identical to friendship with God, either now or in the kingdom. Augustine calls the church a *corpus permixtum* or "mixed body," made up of both the saved and the unsaved; moreover, just as there are profane elements within the church, there are sacred elements outside of it. "Some predestined friends, as yet unknown even to themselves, are concealed even among our most known enemies." The friends and foes of God "are interwoven and intermixed in this era, and await separation at the last judgment" (*City of God* 1.35).

If the boundaries of the church are not the boundaries of salvation, what are? The first letter to Timothy, probably written by a follower of St. Paul, says that God "desires everyone to be saved and to come to the knowledge of the truth" (1 Tim. 2:4). This seems to draw the boundaries as widely as possible: God desires *everyone* to be saved. But Jesus also speaks of the "narrow door" of the kingdom (Luke 13:24), and of how no one comes to the Father except by him (John 14:6), and warns of the fires of hell (Matt. 10:28; 23:33), all of which would seem to draw a more restricted boundary to salvation. We might also ask, does the freedom of human beings extend as far as the possibility of refusing God's offer of salvation? How might it be the case that loss of life in the kingdom is a real possibility, and yet God's universal will for human salvation is not thwarted?

Julian of Norwich struggles with these questions, asking how it could be possible that, as she understood the Bible to teach, some creatures would be damned to hell and yet, as God had said to her in her visions, "all shall be well." She writes, "I had no other answer revealed by our Lord except this: What is impossible to you is not impossible to me. I will preserve my word in all things, and I will make all things well" (*Revelations of Divine Love*, chap. 32). As Julian sees it, our obligation, as in all cases, is to pray "thy will be done" and hold fast to the kindness of God, hoping that God's desire that all be saved would come to pass, without claiming to know whether the freedom of creatures might condition that desire in such a way that some might be lost. The question of who will be saved is one case where a certain reverent agnosticism, a willingness not to know, commends itself.

If the boundary of salvation is not identical with the boundary of the church, and if the former boundary is at least potentially far wider than the latter, why bother with the church? Why would the Spirit call people into such a community, bound together by the visible bonds of religion? Perhaps

be more accurate to say that while Jesus is unfailingly and effectively faithful to his promise to be with his friends, even to the end of the ages (Matt. 28:20), the church sometimes hides that presence rather than revealing it. But the promise endures despite the failures, and the hidden power of the Spirit can burst forth unexpectedly. The kiss that the church exchanges with God in the daily routine of prayer and service can at any moment pass beyond ritual and turn, as Dorothy Day puts it, "to rapture, a burning fire of tenderness and love."

In the winter of 2002 I was on a work-related trip to Florence, Italy. Some will remember that this was a particularly dark time in the world. It was only a few months after the horrific terrorist attacks of September 11, 2001, that had killed nearly three thousand people. The drums of war were beating with ever-increasing intensity, driving toward a war without boundaries, a war that even now is still smoldering. Like many, I was torn between a sense of having to do *something* in response to terroristic violence and a sense of bewilderment as to *what* should be done. The immediate feeling of crisis that had flared up as we watched the twin towers fall had become in me a kind of low-grade fever, sapping my energy and engendering a sense of despair.

One evening I went to the ancient Florentine monastery known as La Badia. It is currently used as a place of worship by the members of the Fraternités Monastiques de Jérusalem, a religious order of men and women, founded in Paris in 1975, that is dedicated to living out the age-old life of monks and nuns within the "desert" of the modern city. The members live together in rented apartments, holding all their property in common, and each works part-time, often in secular employment, to support their religious community. They are particularly devoted to outreach to the religiously unaffiliated, inter-religious dialogue, solidarity with the poor, and the public worship of God. In secular Europe, they are a remarkable "success story," with many young people joining their ranks to live lives of poverty, chastity, and obedience.

As the evening prayer of vespers passed into the celebration of the Eucharist, I was moved by the care and beauty of their liturgy: the harmonized chanting of voices male and female, young and old; the clouds of incense representing the rising of our prayers to God; bodies bent in prayer and standing with upraised hands in praise. We were bound together in an ancient ritual, made into a single worshiping body. After the Eucharistic prayer, by which the Spirit makes the risen Jesus present bodily once more in our midst, and just before we were to be fed by that same risen Jesus in Communion, the priest wished us the peace of Christ. The monks and nuns moved out from their places before the altar into the gathered people to exchange with us the ritual greeting of peace.

A nun clasped both of my hands in hers; she looked into my eyes and spoke one of the handfuls of Italian words that I knew. I knew it because I had seen it on innumerable rainbow-colored banners hanging from windows throughout Italy, banners that seemed like a stillborn desire, a hopeless prayer, as nations marched toward war: *pace*—peace. I responded with that same word: *pace*. Suddenly, I was shaken to my core by an almost physical sensation. I was shaken by the overwhelming conviction that *it's all true*. All of it. In the eyes of this nun, in her voice, in the pressure of her hands around mine, I saw and heard and felt that the good news is true: God is love; love is crucified; Jesus calls us friends; we must love our neighbor; and, even amid the cacophony of the drums of war, the Spirit's voice can still be heard, calling us into a community that embodies God's peace.

War still came. It is with us still. It seems always with us: the war of everyone against everyone, the old story of self-seeking and fear. But even as we endure the flow of time, awaiting redemption, God's kindness grants us moments of vision, signs by which we see through the deadly illusion of false security through violence, when we find the reality of the kingdom lying hidden like treasure in the earth, like a seed growing in a way that is beyond our ordinary ability to see. The vision of this kingdom sustains us as we strive to enter it by clothing the naked, feeding the hungry, visiting the imprisoned, caring for the sick, seeking in them the face of Jesus, the face of crucified love. Though the presence of the kingdom may seem delayed by our own stubbornness and hardness of heart, it is already here through the Spirit who helps us in our weakness, calling us into the body of Christ, and out of that body into the world.

> For there is still a vision for the appointed time;
>   it speaks of the end, and does not lie.
> If it seems to tarry, wait for it;
>   it will surely come, it will not delay.
>   (Hab. 2:3)

Further Reading

- The Letter to the Ephesians. This is either one of Paul's later letters or a letter written by a follower of Paul addressing a community of Christians trying to understand the implications of God's reconciling work among Jew and Greek, slave and free, male and female.

- Dorothy Day, *The Long Loneliness*. This autobiography tells of how Day, a secular anarchist and pacifist, found herself called into a church that she loved even as she called it to deeper faithfulness in living out Jesus's radical message of love for the poor.

Homiletic Epilogue

A sermon for the Sixth Sunday of Easter Season

Corpus Christi Church, Baltimore, Maryland

On Peter's arrival, Cornelius met him, and falling at his feet, worshiped him. But Peter made him get up, saying, "Stand up; I am only a mortal." . . .

Then Peter began to speak to them: "I truly understand that God shows no partiality, but in every nation anyone who fears him and does what is right is acceptable to him." . . .

While Peter was still speaking, the Holy Spirit fell upon all who heard the word. The circumcised believers who had come with Peter were astounded that the gift of the Holy Spirit had been poured out even on the Gentiles, for they heard them speaking in tongues and extolling God. Then Peter said, "Can anyone withhold the water for baptizing these people who have received the Holy Spirit just as we have?" So he ordered them to be baptized in the name of Jesus Christ. Then they invited him to stay for several days (Acts 10:25-26, 34-35, 44-48).

Beloved, let us love one another because love is from God; everyone who loves is born of God and knows God. Whoever does not love does not know God, for God is love. God's love was revealed among us in this way: God sent his only Son into the world so that we might live through him. In this is love, not that we loved God but that he loved us and sent his Son to be the atoning sacrifice for our sins. (1 John 4:7–10)

> As the Father has loved me, so I have loved you; abide in my love. If you keep my commandments, you will abide in my love, just as I have kept my Father's commandments and abide in his love. I have said these things to you so that my joy may be in you, and that your joy may be complete.
>
> This is my commandment, that you love one another as I have loved you. No one has greater love than this, to lay down one's life for one's friends. You are my friends if you do what I command you. I do not call you servants any longer, because the servant does not know what the master is doing; but I have called you friends, because I have made known to you everything that I have heard from my Father. You did not choose me but I chose you. And I appointed you to go and bear fruit, fruit that will last, so that the Father will give you whatever you ask him in my name. I am giving you these commands so that you may love one another. (John 15:9–17)

> What is Christianity all about?
> Some might be inclined
> to answer this question
> by reciting the creed,
> and they would not be wrong,
> because being a Christian

does involve believing certain things.
Others might be inclined to answer
by pointing to certain moral principles,
and, again, they would not be wrong,
because being a Christian
does involve behaving in certain ways.
But what Christianity is about
must be something more
than a collection of beliefs and behaviors;
it must be a mystery that sinks its roots
into the heart of life itself.

This mystery, however,
is mysterious not because it is complicated,
but because it is so simple.
Today's readings from sacred Scripture
constitute together a kind of refresher course,
in five simple lessons,
of what Christianity is all about.

First, God is love.
This has of course become something of a cliché,
so much so that when I typed
"God is . . ." into Google
"God is love" came up
as the second most-popular search item,
right behind "God is good"
(and just ahead of "God is dope" and "God is dead").

Because it has become something of a cliché
we can forget
what a revolutionary notion this was
in the world of antiquity
whose pantheons were populated
by deities that were powerful and crafty,
but not particularly loving.
Yet Christianity says not only that God is loving
but that God is love itself.
St. Augustine wrote that if the entire Bible
contained only the words "God is love"
we should ask for nothing more.

Second, the love that is God
is crucified love.
We know the depth of the mystery of love
because "God sent his only Son into the world
so that we might live through him."
The cross of Jesus shows us
that the love that gives its life for our life
is love that ceaselessly, relentlessly, scandalously
pours itself out.
And it is precisely in not holding itself back,
not hesitating to give itself up,
that this love is
"the atoning sacrifice for our sins"—
that is, it is the life-giving mystery
that we call God,
because there is no greater love than this.

Third, we are called to friendship
with the risen Jesus.
As he says in our Gospel reading,
"I have called you friends . . .
You did not choose me but I chose you."
We are called to friendship with God
not because of anything we are or do
but out of the depth of love
that is the divine mystery
revealed in the cross.
And the resurrection of Jesus,
which we celebrate in every Eucharist,
but especially in this Easter season,
is what makes possible
our ongoing friendship with him,
our continuous abiding in the love that is God.

Fourth, we cannot love God
if we do not love each other.
As the first letter of John puts it,
"Beloved, let us love one another,
because love is from God."
We love God
by loving our neighbor as Jesus loved us:
loving both friend and enemy,
laying down our lives for one another
in ways dramatic and ordinary:
in acts of sacrifice and of gratitude,
in patience, honesty,

forbearance, and generosity,
for "whoever does not love
does not know God."

Fifth, we live our love out from
the community created by the Spirit.
While we are called to a universal love
of both friend and enemy,
we live that love from the heart of the church.
And the Spirit, who is the divine mystery of love
that shows no partiality,
gathers friends of Jesus together
into an unlikely and motley crew of lovers.
At any given place and time
we have no idea
what this community will look like,
except we know it will be filled with people
whom we would not have chosen to love
if we were not friends of Jesus.
Peter, in our first reading,
would never have chosen friendship
with a Gentile like Cornelius.
But the Spirit moved, and there it was.
Who was Peter to argue with the Spirit?
Look around you.
These are the people
with whom God has called you
into friendship in Christ
through the waters of baptism:

men and women,
old and young,
black and white,
conservative and liberal,
gay and straight,
native and immigrant,
courageous and cowardly,
stupid and smart,
handsome and hideous,
saints and sinners,
and every type of human animal
who doesn't quite know *what* they are,
except they know this one thing:
the God who is love has called them
into his crucified love.
Look around you.
Who are we to argue with the Spirit?

God is love.
The love that is God is crucified love.
We are called to friendship with the risen Jesus.
We cannot love God if we do not love each other.
We live our love out
from the community created by the Spirit.
That is it.
That is what Christianity is all about.
Now believe it and live it
as if your life depended on it,
because it does.

Works Cited

Biblical quotations are taken from the *New Revised Standard Version*. For ancient and medieval works, I have not always followed the translations given below but sometimes give my own translations. These are intended for readers who want to read more deeply in one or more of the works cited.

Anselm of Canterbury. *Proslogion*. In *The Major Works*. Edited by Brian Davies and Gillian Evans. Oxford: Oxford University Press, 1998.

Aristotle. *The Nicomachean Ethics*. Translated by W. D. Ross and J. O. Urmson. In *The Complete Works of Aristotle: The Revised Oxford Translation*. Volume 2, edited by Jonathan Barnes. Princeton, NJ: Princeton University Press, 1984.

Augustine of Hippo. *Concerning the City of God against the Pagans*. Translated by Henry Bettenson. London: Penguin, 1984.

———. *Confessions*. Translated by Henry Chadwick. Oxford: Oxford University Press, 1991.

———. Epistle 130. In *Letters*. Volume 2. Translated by Wilfrid Parsons. Vol. 18 of Fathers of the Church. Washington, DC: Catholic University of America Press, 1953.

———. *The Trinity* (*De Trinitate*). Translated by Stephen McKenna. Washington, DC: Catholic University of America Press, 1963.

Benedict XVI. *God Is Love: Deus caritas est.* San Francisco: Ignatius Press, 2006.

Catherine of Siena. *The Dialogue.* Translated by Suzanne Noffke. Mahwah, NJ: Paulist Press, 1980.

Chaucer, Geoffrey. *The Canterbury Tales.* Translated by Peter Levi. Oxford: Oxford University Press, 1985.

Day, Dorothy. "Bread for the Hungry." Address at the Forty-First International Eucharistic Congress, Philadelphia, August 6, 1976. http://www.catholicworker.org/dorothyday/articles/258.pdf.

———. *The Long Loneliness.* New York: Harper, 1952.

Dostoyevsky, Fyodor. *The Brothers Karamazov.* Translated by Richard Pevear and Larissa Volokhonsky. New York: Farrar, Straus and Giroux, 2002.

Ellacuría, Ignacio. *Essays on History, Liberation, and Salvation.* Translated by Michael Lee. Maryknoll, NY: Orbis Books, 2013.

Gregory of Nyssa. *The Life of Moses.* Translated by Everett Ferguson and Abraham J. Malherbe. New York: Paulist Press, 1978.

Hegel, Georg Wilhelm Friedrich. *The Philosophy of History.* Translated by J. Sibree. New York: Dover, 1956.

Hobbes, Thomas. *Leviathan.* Cambridge: Cambridge University Press, 1996.

Ignatius of Antioch. *Letter to the Romans* in *Early Christian Writings.* Translated by Maxwell Staniforth. Harmondsworth, UK: Penguin Books, 1987.

John Chrysostom. *On Matthew.* In *Nicene and Post-Nicene Fathers.* Volume 10, edited by Philip Schaff. Peabody, MA: Hendrickson, 1994.

Julian of Norwich. *Revelations of Divine Love*. Translated by Elizabeth Spearing. London: Penguin Books, 1998.

King, Martin Luther, Jr. *Strength to Love*. Minneapolis: Fortress Press, 2010.

Newman, John Henry. *Apologia pro Vita Sua*. London: Longman, Roberts & Green, 1864.

Nietzsche, Friedrich. *The Joyful Wisdom (Joyful Science)*. Translated by Thomas Common. New York: Macmillan, 1924.

———. *On the Genealogy of Morals/Ecce Homo*. Translated by Walter Kaufmann and R. J. Hollingdale. New York: Vintage Books, 1967.

———. *Twilight of the Idols/The Anti-Christ*. Translated by R. J. Hollingdale. London: Penguin Books, 1990.

O'Driscoll, Mary, ed. *Catherine of Siena: Passion for Truth, Compassion for Humanity*. Hyde Park, NY: New City Press, 1993.

Pieper, Josef. "On Love." In *Faith, Hope, Love*, translated by Richard and Clara Winston. San Francisco: Ignatius Press, 1997.

Richard of St. Victor. *On the Trinity (De Trinitate)*. Translated by Christopher P. Evans. In *Trinity and Creation*, ed. Boyd Taylor Coolman and Dale M. Coulter. Hyde Park, NY: New City Press, 2011.

Thérèse of Lisieux. *Story of a Soul: The Autobiography of St. Thérèse of Lisieux*. 2nd ed. Translated by John Clarke. Washington, DC: Institute of Carmelite Studies, 1976.

Thomas Aquinas. *Summa Theologica (Summa theologiae)*. 5 vols. Translated by the Fathers of the English Dominican Province. Westminster, MD: Christian Classics, 1981.